ADVANCED SEARCH AND RESCUE

Senior Author
Craig Bannerman

Contributing Authors:
Steve Foster
Darwin Glassford
William Johnson
Larry Jones
Tom Millen
Larry Pugh
Kevin Rolfe
Jim Stumpf
Jim Taylor
Gary Williams
Ed Wolff
Art Wolff

Editors
Craig Bannerman and Steve Foster

Illustrations by Larry Pierson, Jr.

Copyright 1997 National Association for Search and Rescue
Fourth Printing, 2000

INTRODUCTION

In 1991, the National Association for Search and Rescue recognized a need to provide a measurable standard of performance for search resources in the United States. This process was implemented through the SAR Technician Certification Program which began testing in 1992. The initial levels of certification developed were SAR Tech III & II. The standards for these certifications were based on the skills and knowledge taught in the Fundamentals of Search and Rescue course, offered by NASAR.

In 1993, NASAR began to develop the next level of certification, the SAR Tech I / Crewleader III standard. This level of certification is based on the Crewleader level of responder. To prepare the Candidate for this level of certification, NASAR also began developing the Advanced Search & Rescue text and course teaching outlines. This text assists the Crewleader in obtaining the knowledge and skills needed to enable the individual to responsibly lead a SAR crew. Topics such as Land Navigation, Safety, Hazardous Terrain, and Search Techniques and Tactics allow the searcher to prepare for the Certification exam. The topics and information needed for this document were recommended by many of NASAR's Instructors and Coordinators.

The pilot ADSAR (Advanced Search and Rescue) course was held in Asheboro, NC at Randolph Community College during March, 1996. The course was followed by the first SAR Tech I / Crewleader III exam and certification, in which thirteen candidates from around the nation were certified.

Many individuals contributed to the writing of this text and the process of testing the standard and course work. NASAR owes many thanks to the following people for their contributions to the text. Steve Foster, Darwin Glassford, William Johnson, Larry Jones, Tom Millen, Larry Pugh, Kevin Rolfe, Jim Stumpf, Jim Taylor, Gary Williams, Ed Wolff, Mylea Wade and Art Wolff. NASAR also wishes to express a debt of gratitude to Randolph Community College and the Randolph County Search & Rescue team, for the support of the first course and exam.

It is the intent of those of us who have worked to put this text together that it provide a starting point for crewleaders to continue to learn and grow in SAR knowledge and skills. Nothing within this text should be taken as the only knowledge or technique to use in SAR. We have attempted to provide the most current methods of operation based on all of our experience. Every contributor to this text is actively involved in operational or management levels of search with the exception of Jim Stumpf, whose expertise in ICS topics and management have proven to be invaluable to SAR responders and educators.

Our hope is that by improving our level of response through this course, we may benefit those who rely on us in an emergency.

That Others May Live

Craig Bannerman

Table of Contents

Chapter 1	- Incident Command System Management	page 1
Chapter 2	- Small Unit Leadership	page 19
Chapter 3	- Fitness for the Crew Leader	page 29
Chapter 4	- Crew Safety	page 37
Chapter 5	- Ready Pack for SAR Technician I/Crewleader III -	page 53
Chapter 6	- Maps, Symbology, and Navigation	page 63
Chapter 7	- Search Techniques and Tactics	page 83
Chapter 8	- Briefing and Debriefing	page 117
Chapter 9	- Hazardous Terrain Safety	page 127
Chapter 10	- Stress Management	page 139
Summary		page 145

ICS MANAGEMENT

OBJECTIVES

A. The student shall explain the relationship of the ICS modular concept as it relates to a typical search incident.
   1. The five (5) functional sections
   2. The four (4) management levels of the operations section

B. The student shall identify the resources commonly managed under an ICS system during a SAR incident.

C. The student shall define the following components of comprehensive resource management:
   1. Single Resource
   2. Task Forces
   3. Strike Teams

D. The student shall define the three (3) status conditions placed on resources when using comprehensive resource management.
   1. Available
   2. Assigned
   3. Out of service

E. The student shall correctly explain the information required for each entry on the ICS 204 form, Assignment List.

F. The student shall correctly explain the information required for each entry on ICS 214 form, Unit Log.

G. The student shall explain the use of an ICS 204 and 214 form, as it relates to the crew and the managers of a SAR incident.

H. The student shall list and describe the components of an Incident Action Plan.

I. The student shall describe the relationship of the IAP to the crewleader and other SAR resources.

J. The student shall identify the information used to complete an ICS form 202, 203, 204, 205, and 206.

ICS MANAGEMENT

The nature of any search or rescue management structure is determined by many factors. The severity of the problem, urgency of the situation and the technical requirements of the search will influence how large a management team will be needed. The Incident Command System is expandable and will operate the simplest to the most complex incidents. ICS has tiered functional levels and distinctive titles identifying those responsible at each level. A simple search for a lost subject may require no more than an Incident Commander to direct the searchers. A severe injury and complex rescue problem may require many Command or General Staff members operating as a team. The Incident Command System is **flexible**.

Another incident might begin as a complex technical rescue to move a seriously traumatized patient. After investigating the situation, it may be determined, other Crews will be needed to start searching for additional members of the patient's party. In this case the person who had been titled the "Rescue Crewleader" has now the added responsibility for a larger number of personnel operating in different parts of the search area with different areas of responsibility. Before the good manager looses his span of control, he/she should establish Crews/Teams for each function. The manager would now be referred to as the Strike Team Leader, Task Force Leader, or Division/Group Supervisor.

In the ICS the expansion of supervisory/management responsibility is primarily driven by the recommended 5:1 span of control. That is, when more than five Crews, Teams, or Task Forces are necessary they should be formed into functional groups or geographical divisions and Division/Group Supervisors assigned. Finally, if more than five Groups are assigned the incident should be branched by geographical or functional assignments. Branch Directors are assigned at this level of management. These functional areas all fall under the Operations Section and are supervised by the Operations Section Chief.

Each search and rescue incident will have an Incident Command System structure built for that particular incident. Similarly, the person at any level of function or management must keep ahead of the problem. The problem in the case of management is usually building a system to maintain an acceptable span of control and thus preventing confusion.

There are five major organizational functions (rather than specific persons) common to every rescue regardless of the size of the mission. The five basic functions are:

Command
Operations
Logistics
Planning
Finance/Administration

The **Command** function is obvious and functions at the top of the chain of responsibility. The Incident Commander is the person who must accept the ultimate outcome for the incident. This individual develops the overall incident objectives, strategies and manages all activities that occur on the incident. Delegation to other personnel in the various functional roles places the task completion burden on others.

During small operations one person may assume responsibility for all five functions and direct the entire incident. A diagram of a small incident is shown in **Figure 1.1**.

Chapter 1 - ICS Management

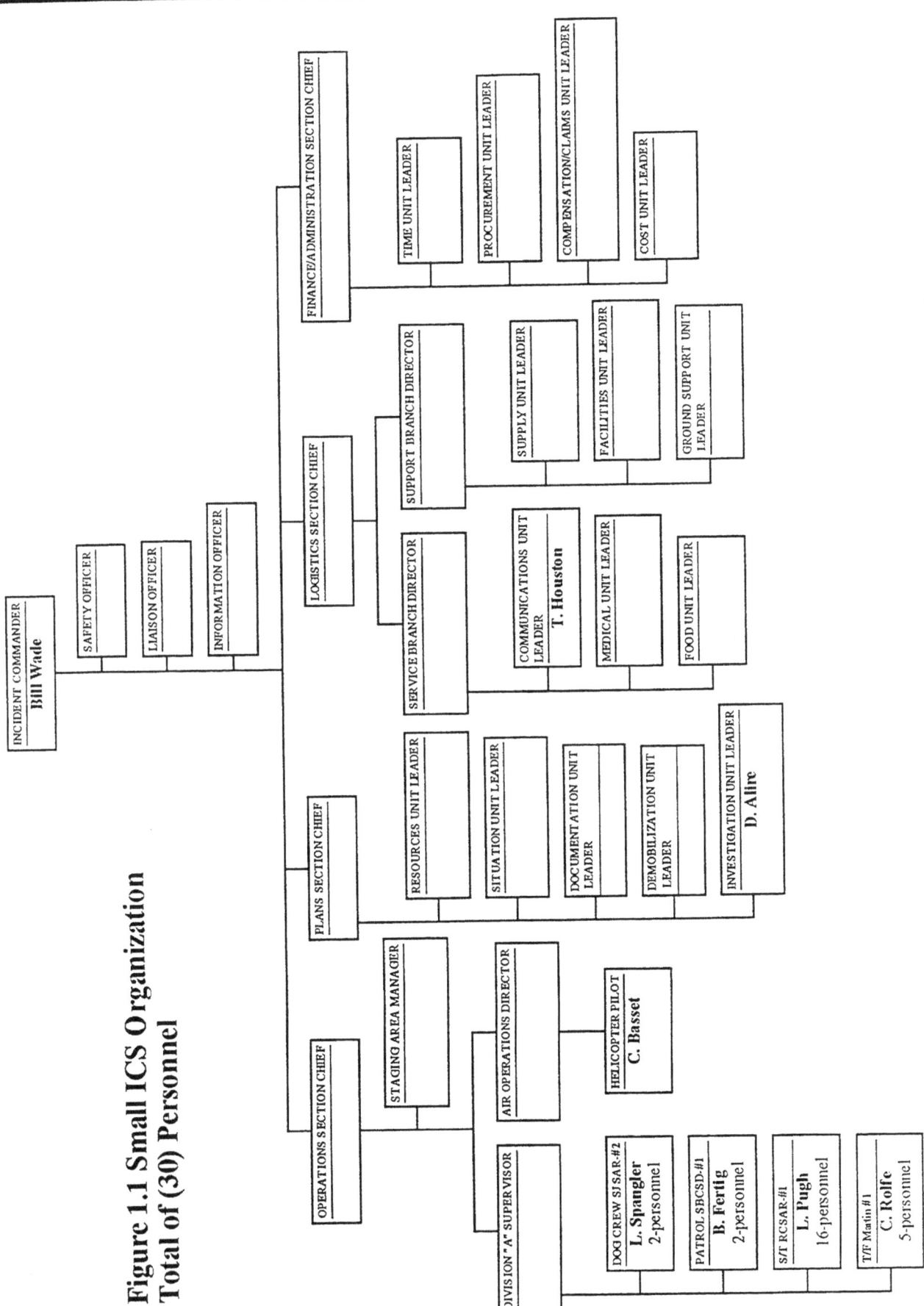

Figure 1.1 Small ICS Organization Total of (30) Personnel

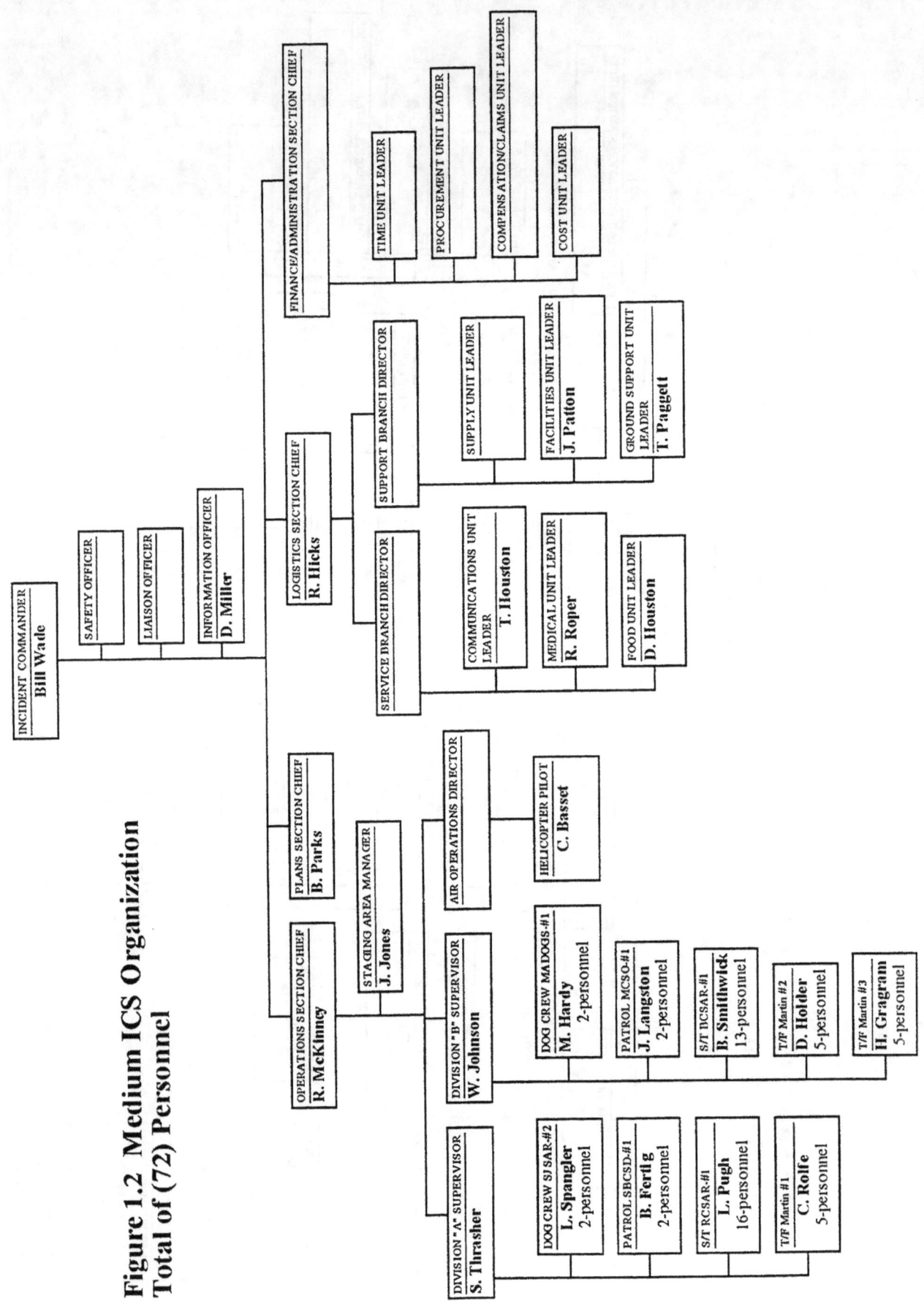

**Figure 1.2 Medium ICS Organization
Total of (72) Personnel**

If the incident becomes a major rescue, the management system grows. A manageable span of control is maintained. As the incident becomes more complex the person responsible for Command may wish to place a person in charge of each function with personnel to direct. This is shown in the **Figure 1.2**.

With increasing demands on the management system, standard positions are established and more levels are added in the functions as needed.

Operations Section consists of four levels of management. The levels include the section, branch, division or group, and task force, strike team, or crew levels.

The Operations Section Chief is a member of the General Staff and responsible for the management of all operations directly applicable to the primary mission. The Operations Section Chief also determines tactics and directs the preparation of operational plans, requests or releases and reports to the Incident Commander. Additional responsibilities include:

- Obtain briefing from the Incident Commander.
- Develop the tactics for the Incident Action Plan.
- Brief and assign operations personnel with the Incident Action Plan.
- Supervise operations.
- Determine need and request additional resources.
- Assemble and disassemble units and teams assigned to the Operations Section.
- Supervise subordinates.

Below the organizational level of **Branch Director** alternate titles may be shown. For example, when dealing with functions rather than geographical areas a **Division Supervisor** becomes a functional **Group Supervisor**, i.e. "Rescue Group Supervisor". The several **Crews, Strike Teams, or Task Forces** assigned to this function would have the Group Supervisor as a Leader. Bear in mind that the span of control drives the organizational structure. A Group Supervisor can manage up to five Crews, Strike Teams, or Task Forces, each operating under different functional areas on the incident.

The **Staging Area** is developed when resources need to be placed in an **Available Status** (3 minute, ready-alert). The Staging Area Manager is responsible for all activities that occur within the Staging Area.

Resources commonly managed under an ICS system during a SAR incident are limited only by the imagination of the Incident Commander and the specific needs of the incident. It is preferable to have fully trained and qualified people but this is not always possible. Publications such as the Field Operations Guide outline checklists to be used by people who perform in the ICS positions. Experience of the personnel used and the background and experience of the Incident Commander may have a bearing on personnel assigned.

OPERATIONAL RESOURCES

Operational resources within the Incident Command System are managed as single resources, task forces and strike teams.

Single Resource (S) - A single resource can be any piece of equipment, any person, or any small number of persons who is assigned to perform an operational task. For instance, a Type II Search Crew consisting of three persons is considered a single resource. It usually takes at least three persons for the Type II Search Crew to be functional.

Strike Teams (S/T) - A Strike Team is two or more of the same kind and type of resources. During SAR operations strike teams may be established on scene but should really be predesignated. A Strike Team Leader is designated to provide supervision. Common communication between the leader and the strike team resources is a must. A typical Type II Search Crew Strike Team would consist of three Type II Search Crews and a leader.

Task Forces (T/F) - A Task Force is any combination of resources assigned for a specific job on an incident. Span of control is the major governing factor on the number of single resources deployed into a Task Force. A Task Force Leader is designated to provide supervision. Common communication between the Leader and the Task Force members is a must. An example of a Task Force commonly used on a search would be combining a Search Crew and a Search Dog Crew to include a Task Force Leader.

There are three status conditions placed on resources when using the comprehensive resource management system, designed by ICS for any resource on an incident.

Available - An available resource is one that can be assigned to the incident. These resources would normally be located in Staging Areas. They could also be located at other facilities on the incident. These resources have been briefed and are on a three-minute standby. In other words, these resources can be enroute to the assigned areas within three minutes.

Assigned - Assigned resources are committed to carrying out specific duties at the incident. Once assigned, the resource is unavailable to accomplish other tasks unless approved by their supervisor.

Out of Service - This status occurs for several reasons. First, the resource may be resting because of previous incident activities. The resource may have a mechanical deficiency, such as a breakdown, that would prohibit the use of the resource. In some cases, a resource may be out of service because there are insufficient personnel available within a unit to have it operate efficiently.

ICS FORMS

ICS 204 Form, Assignment List - There are ten (10) separate blocks of information required on the ICS 204 form, Assignment List. Many of these blocks may require multiple entries. The Resources Unit Leader is responsible for the completion of the form at the conclusion of the Planning Meeting. The ICS 204 form is included as part of the Incident Action Plan. The IAP provides the written direction for all operational portions of the incident. It provides specific direction and expectations to all assigned. See **Figure 1.3 - ICS Form 204**.

1. **Branch** - Used to designate which Branch the assignment refers to. If not used, put N/A in the field to let the reader know there was no omission.
2. **Division/Group** - Indicate the appropriate geographical or functional area the assignment refer to.
3. **Incident name, date and time prepared** - These entries are common to all ICS forms.
4. **Operational Period** - Refers to the date and time of the Operational Period planned.
5. **Operations Personnel** - Designates, by name, the Operations Personnel assigned.
6. **Resources Assigned this Period** - Provides six columns that list all personnel assigned to the specific Division/Group. The resource designator is entered to identify the unit. During SAR operations the form can be used at the Crew, Strike Team or Task Force level. At this level the leader's name and all personnel names would be entered. If used at the Division/Group level, only the unit leader should be identified as well as the total number of personnel assigned. A yes or no answer will satisfy the column that asks about Transportation needed. The drop-off and pickup points are important to let personnel know the expected duration of the assignment.
7. **Control Operations** - This portion of the form outlines the specific expectations of the unit or units assigned to this Division or Group for the Operational Period. During SAR operations, these expectations may include:

Chapter 1 - ICS Management

- What segment to search or where to search.
- Route to the search segment.
- Type of search (Hasty, Efficient, Thorough, Sign Cutting, Confinement, etc.)
- How to search or what techniques are to be used.
- General direction to search.
- The expected Probability of Detection.
- Search starting and ending locations.
- The estimated time needed to accomplish the search.

8. **Special Instructions** - As the heading implies, any special information on hazards, tools, equipment and anything else applicable would be listed here.

- Examples
- Map coordinates of Drop Off Point and Pick Up Point.
- Segment size, boundaries, terrain and major landmarks.
- Possible clues and clue considerations.
- Communications considerations.
- SOPs if subject is located.
- Medical emergencies.
- Equipment considerations.
- Hazard considerations.
- Family and media considerations.

9. **Division/Group Communications Summary** - All communications planning for the incident is the responsibility of the Communications Unit Leader or the Logistics Section Chief. This entry merely summarizes information regarding specific communication for the Division or Group referred to.
10. **Signature Blocks** - provide the signature of the Resources Unit Leader, responsible for the completion of the form and the approval of the Planning Section Chief.

ICS 214 Form, Unit Log - All Crew/Strike Team/Task Force and Unit Leaders, Division/Group Supervisors, Command and General Staff personnel are required to complete the ICS 214 form, Unit Log for each Operational Period. Completed forms are filed with the Documentation Unit Leader and become a part of the complete documentation saved for the incident. The ICS 214 is often attached to the ICS 204 form and is used as a debriefing document for each crew assigned at the end of the Operational Period. There are eight entries required for the ICS 214 form. **See Figure 1.4 - ICS Form 214.**

1. **Incident Name** - All incidents need to be named or numbered for statistical purposes.
2. **Date prepared** - MM/DD/YYYY.
3. **Time Prepared** - self explanatory.
4. **Unit Name/Designator** - The name of your team or the position you are filling on the incident.
5. **Unit Leader (name and position)** - Indicates the name of the person managing the unit.
6. **Operational Period** - The time period scheduled for the execution of the assignment.
7. **Personnel Roster Assigned** - These three columns provide spaces to list the people assigned in your area of responsibility.
8. **Activity Log** - The time column indicates the time the event took place. The major event column is where a brief but complete narrative of the event is documented.

The Incident Action Plan (IAP) is used to provide guidance and accountability of all personnel assigned. The plan does not have to be written for smaller incidents and can be provided verbally to all assigned. On larger complex incidents, a written plan is a must. The Plan includes the following ICS Forms: ICS-202, 203, 204 (one for each Division or Group and may include Crew/Strike Team/Task Force), 205 and 206.

The plan may also include maps, a Traffic Plan, ICS-214, Subject Profile, Copies of footprints or victim's photo, etc.

The IAP provides direction and articulates the overall Incident Objectives to all leaders and resources. In addition, the IAP provides information on all resources assigned to an incident. This will enable adjoining resources to better communicate, to share personnel or equipment and optimize personnel working in the same search segment or adjoining segments.

The information used to complete an Incident Action Plan is obtained as the result of the Planning Meeting. All Command and General Staff participate in this planning process. The ICS forms 202, 203, 205, and 206 are completed as part of the IAP from the information gathered and discussed at this meeting. It is the Planning Section's responsibility to complete the IAP once the Incident Commander has approved the tactical plan submitted by the Operations Section Chief during the Planning Meeting.

ICS Form 202, Incident Objectives Form- This form becomes the cover page for the IAP and serves the primary purpose to articulate the over-all incident objectives developed by the Incident Commander. These objectives must be broad enough to be used for the entire incident. There is also space on the form to provide a brief and general weather forecast and safety messages. The ICS 202 also provides a list of the content of the entire IAP. The Planning Section Chief is responsible for the preparation of the form. The Incident Commander approves the ICS 202 and the entire IAP. See **Figure 1.5 - ICS Form 202, Incident Objectives Form.**

ICS 203, Organization Assignment List- Provides the names and titles of all personnel assigned to the incident. The Resources Unit Leader is responsible to complete the information that is included. See **Figure 1.6 - ICS 203, Organization Assignment List.**

ICS 205, Incident Radio Communications Plan- The form is completed by the Communications Unit Leader or Logistics Section Chief and provides information to all personnel assigned on the various radio frequencies in use on the incident. In addition to the frequencies for command, tactical, support and ground-to-air, it identifies the specific functions on the incident who use the nets. See **Figure 1.7 - ICS 205, Incident Radio Communications Plan.**

ICS 206, Medical Plan- The Medical Plan is developed by the Medical Unit Leader or Logistics Section Chief and reviewed by the Safety Officer. The intent of the information in this form is to provide a medical plan for incident assigned personnel. It is not designed for the victim. Information on the form will show the location of incident medical aid stations and ambulance assignments on the incident. It will also exhibit off-site hospitals and ambulance services. The form provides information to all assigned personnel on the actual procedures to be used in the event of an accident or injury to someone participating on the incident. See **Figure 1.8 - ICS 206, Medical Plan**

Chapter 1 - ICS Management

1. BRANCH	2. DIVISION/GROUP	ASSIGNMENT LIST ICS 204
3. INCIDENT NAME		4. OPERATIONAL PERIOD DATE_____ TIME

5. OPERATIONS PERSONNEL

OPERATIONS CHIEF _____ DIVISION/GROUP SUPERVISOR_____

BRANCH DIRECTOR _____ AIR OPERATIONS _____

STRIKE TEAM/TASK FORCE RESOURCE DESIGNATOR	CREW LEADER/MEMBERS	NUMBER PERSONS	TRANS NEEDED	DROP OFF POINT/TIME	PICK UP POINT/TIME

7. TACTICAL OPERATIONS

8. SPECIAL INSTRUCTIONS

9. DIVISION/GROUP COMMUNICATIONS SUMMARY

FUNCTION		FREQ.	SYSTEM	CHANNEL	FUNCTION		FREQ.	SYSTEM	CHANNEL
COMMAND	LOCAL				SUPPORT	LOCAL			
	REPEAT					REPEAT			
DIVISION/GROUP TACTICAL					GROUND TO AIR				
PREPARED BY (RESOURCE UNIT LEADER					APPROVED BY (PLANNING SECTION CHIEF)			DATE	TIME

Figure 1.3 ICS Form 204

Chapter 1 - ICS Management

1. BRANCH	2. DIVISION / GROUP	ASSIGNMENT LIST	№ 20495
N/A	A		

3. INCIDENT NAME	4. OPERATIONAL PERIOD	
Salinas Search	DATE 2/02/90	7TH TIME 0600-1800

5. OPERATIONS PERSONNEL

OPERATIONS CHIEF: Randy McKinney   DIVISION / GROUP SUPERVISOR: Jim Taylor

BRANCH DIRECTOR: N/A

6. RESOURCES ASSIGNED THIS PERIOD

STRIKE TEAM / TASK FORCE / RESOURCE DESIGNATOR	LEADER	NUMBER PERSONS	TRANS. NEEDED	DROP OFF PT./ TIME	PICK UP PT./ TIME
T/F Salinas #1	J. Rogers	5	Y	0700	1730
BCSAR C#1	S. Godfrey				
	J. Winters				
	J. Goad				
DOGSE C#2	L. Lightsey				

7. CONTROL OPERATIONS - A. Perform a (Hasty, Efficient, Thorough, Sign-Cut, Confinement, Etc.) in Seg. # (Route, Etc.) using a (5-Guide Right on Stream-20 m.). B. General direction to search. C. Expected POD. Search starting point (Coordinates). D. Search ending point (Coordinates). Estimate time to complete search.

Perform an "Efficient Type" search of Segment #6 using a "Critical Spacing of One" for BCSAR C#1 while allowing DOGSE C#2 to search ahead. Starting from the LKP (1836/7741) search in a general direction of East to Linville River (1801/7650). Expected PODcum is 70%. Estimate to complete the search is 5 hours.

8. SPECIAL INSTRUCTIONS -
A. Know the location of your Drop-Off-Point(Coordinates) and the route to it.
B. Know your search area (Size, Boundaries, Terrain, Major Landmarks, Distances(Paces), and Directions of Travel.
C. Know the location of your Pick-Up-Point(Coordinates) and indicating landmarks.
D. Brief crew members to individual assignments (Compass, Pace, Radio).
E. Review with crew members:
   (1) Subject profile and possible clues.
   (2) Terrain and landmarks within the search segment.
   (3) Crew objectives.
   (4) Individual equipment required.

CLUE CONSIDERATIONS - Mark and record all possible clues. Report all known clues to CP. Ask CP for instructions concerning the handling of clues.

COMMUNICATIONS CONSIDERATIONS - Report your location every hour.

SUBJECT LOCATION SOPs - A-100 if subject does not require any assistance; A-200 if subject requires medical assistance and evacuation; A-300 if subject is deceased.

MEDICAL EMERGENCIES - Refer Incident Medical Plan.

EQUIPMENT CONSIDERATIONS - Be sure to take extra clothes, 2 qts. of water and food for lunch.

HAZARD CONSIDERATIONS - Watch footing due to wet leaves and steep terrain.

FAMILY AND MEDIA CONSIDERATIONS - Family and friends will be at Incident Base.

9. DIVISION / GROUP COMMUNICATIONS SUMMARY

	FUNCTION		FREQ.	SYSTEM	CHAN.	FUNCTION		FREQ.	SYSTEM	CHAN.
1	COMMAND	LOCAL	155.280	Rescue	N/A	SUPPORT	LOCAL		CB	20
		REPEAT	N/A				REPEAT			
	DIV./ GROUP TACTICAL		46.50	EM	N/A	GROUND TO AIR				

PREPARED BY (RESOURCE UNIT LDR.)	APPROVED BY (PLANNING SECT. CH.)	DATE	TIME
Sandra Smith	Bobby Parks	02/02/90	0400

ICS 204 (1-82)

Figure 1.3 ICS Form 204, Example

Chapter 1 - ICS Management

	1. INCIDENT NAME	2. DATE PREPARED	3. TIME PREPARED
UNIT LOG			
4. UNIT NAME/DESIGNATORS.	5. UNIT LEADER (NAME AND POSITION)	6. OPERATIONAL PERIOD	

7. **PERSONNEL ROSTER ASSIGNED**

NAME	ICS POSITION	HOME BASE

8. **ACTIVITY LOG** (CONTINUE ON REVERSE)

TIME	MAJOR EVENTS

NFES 1337

Figure 1.4 ICS Form 214

TIME	MAJOR EVENTS

214 ICS 5-80	9. PREPARED BY (NAME AND POSITION)

Figure 1.4 ICS Form 214, Part 2

Chapter 1 - ICS Management

INCIDENT OBJECTIVES	1. INCIDENT NAME	2. DATE PREPARED	3. TIME PREPARED

4. OPERATIONAL PERIOD (DATE/TIME)

5. GENERAL CONTROL OBJECTIVES FOR THE INCIDENT (INCLUDE ALTERNATIVES.)

6. WEATHER FORECAST FOR OPERATIONAL PERIOD

7. GENERAL/SAFETY MESSAGE

8. ATTACHMENTS (✓ IF ATTACHED)

- ☐ ORGANIZATION LIST (ICS 203)
- ☐ DIVISION ASSIGNMENT LISTS (ICS 204)
- ☐ COMMUNICATIONS PLAN (ICS 205)
- ☐ MEDICAL PLAN (ICS 206)
- ☐ INCIDENT MAP
- ☐ TRAFFIC PLAN
- ☐ _____
- ☐ _____
- ☐ _____

202 ICS 3/80 | 9. PREPARED BY (PLANNING SECTION CHIEF) | 10. APPROVED BY (INCIDENT COMMANDER)

NFES 1326

Figure 1.5 - ICS Form 202, Incident Objectives Form

Figure 1.6 - ICS 203, Organization Assignment List

INCIDENT RADIO COMMUNICATIONS PLAN	1. INCIDENT NAME	2. DATE/TIME PREPARED	3. OPERATIONAL PERIOD DATE/TIME

4. BASIC RADIO CHANNEL UTILIZATION

SYSTEM/CACHE	CHANNEL	FUNCTION	FREQUENCY/TONE	ASSIGNMENT	REMARKS

205 ICS 9/86 NFES 1330	5. PREPARED BY (COMMUNICATIONS UNIT)

Figure 1.7- ICS 205, Incident Radio Communications Plan

MEDICAL PLAN	1. INCIDENT NAME	2. DATE PREPARED	3. TIME PREPARED	4. OPERATIONAL PERIOD	

5. INCIDENT MEDICAL AID STATIONS

MEDICAL AID STATIONS	LOCATION	PARAMEDICS	
		YES	NO

6. TRANSPORTATION

A. AMBULANCE SERVICES

NAME	ADDRESS	PHONE	PARAMEDICS	
			YES	NO

B. INCIDENT AMBULANCES

NAME	LOCATION	PARAMEDICS	
		YES	NO

7. HOSPITALS

NAME	ADDRESS	TRAVEL TIME		PHONE	HELIPAD		BURN CENTER	
		AIR	GRND		YES	NO	YES	NO

8. MEDICAL EMERGENCY PROCEDURES

9. PREPARED BY (MEDICAL UNIT LEADER)	10. REVIEWED BY (SAFETY OFFICER)

206 ICS 8/78
NFES 1331

Figure 1.8 - ICS 206, Medical Plan

Chapter 1 - ICS Management

REVIEW QUESTIONS

1. The manageable span-of-control for the Incident Command System is?
   _____

2. The 5 functional sections of the Incident Command System are?
   _____   _____
   _____   _____
   _____

3. Staging areas are under the control of the _____ Section Chief.

4. _____ is responsible for developing the Incident Action Plan.

5. The ICS forms that make up the Incident Action Plan include:
   _____   _____
   _____   _____
   _____

6. ICS form #214 is also called? _____

7. The three status conditions used for resources are? _____
   _____   _____

8. _____ is responsible for determining the Incident Objectives.

9. ICS form #206 is developed for who? _____

10. The smallest number of personnel and equipment that can be assigned is a definition of a?
    _____

11. Differing types of resources with common communications and a leader that are assembled for an assignment is a definition of a?
    _____

12. Same type resources with common communications and a leader assembled for an assignment is a definition of a?
    _____

NOTES:

SMALL UNIT LEADERSHIP

OBJECTIVES

A. The student will be able to list and explain ten (10) of the character traits of a good leader.

B. The student will be able to list and explain eight (8) of the principles of leadership.

C. The student will be able to list and explain the six (6) elements of crew leading procedures.

D. The student shall explain the following:
   1. Conflict Management
   2. Situational Management
   3. Supervisory Techniques
   4. Motivational Techniques

SMALL UNIT LEADERSHIP

Leadership is the art of imposing one's will upon others in such a manner as to command their respect, their confidence and their whole-hearted cooperation. A leader is someone who is chartered to complete certain tasks by applying the human resources at his or her disposal. What it takes to be a leader and then what is necessary to lead people is a crucial element in being a small unit leader, or strike team/task force leader in a SAR mission.

LEADERSHIP TRAITS

There are 16 leadership traits you may employ once you begin to use the principles listed above. Remember the way you see yourself is not necessarily the way your subordinates will see you. When you review the below listed traits, be honest with yourself. Just as important as feeling the courage inside you, is the need for that courage to be seen by the people you lead.

COURAGE
Courage is not necessarily charging enemy fire against all odds. Courage is taking risks in the field and elsewhere while acting calmly and firmly even in the most stressful situations. Courage is standing up for what you or you and your crew believe is right regardless of what others may think. Courage is assuming responsibility for your mistakes and for your decisions. Do not blame your work on your supervisor or the people you supervise. Courage directs you to apply yourself full-bore to the mission assignment even in the face of adverse conditions. Courage means correcting crew members at that moment whenever needed.

BEARING
Bearing is best defined as control. You achieve this by setting and maintaining high standards of appearance and performance. A good leader avoids using excessive profanity and controls his voice and actions so that extremes of emotion do not affect your crew members and their performance, except when carefully calculated to do so.

DECISIVENESS
When time permits, a leader studies alternatives and selects the best course of action. A good leader is able to scan alternatives quickly and make fast decisions when time is crucial. The best leader knows when not to make a decision.

DEPENDABILITY
Being on time when you are told to be somewhere or when you say you will be there is an example of being dependable. In the same light, completing tasks you have been assigned or you have chosen to do in a complete and timely manner is a demonstration of dependability. Dependability is a good trait for a leader to share with and insist on from the crew members.

ENDURANCE
As for the crew member, the ability to perform physical and mental tasks under stress and for extended periods of time, with little discomfort, are just as important for the crewleader. The crewleader sets the pace and this must include the ability to perform at peak level throughout the entire assignment.

ENTHUSIASM
Leaders need to demonstrate both orally and by actions a good positive attitude. A leader never criticizes others or management in front of crew members. You need to explain to subordinates why they are performing certain tasks in ways they accept and understand. Leaders need to strive for and insist upon self-initiative from crew members in order to complete assignments as a team. Good leaders emphasize and re-emphasize the successes of their subordinates as a motivator for future successes.

HUMILITY

The leader who lacks humility is self-centered and not a true leader. He is a lone person who has set himself apart from the crew. As a leader, you must give credit to your crew members when they perform well. Emphasize to them they are important to the assignment. The good leader uses phrases such as, "we did well," not, "I did well."

HUMOR

A good leader is still human and should reflect the quality of humor when appropriate. Laugh when something is humorous. Leaders should show they are having fun doing their job; your crew members will reflect this in their own performance. Joking, when the stress hits hardest, is a good way to break the tension and refocus the team.

INITIATIVE

A leader who has initiative has the capability to plan ahead. He is able to make decisions and take action in situations in the absence of direct supervision. A good leader will always look ahead and seek out better ways to accomplish goals.

INTEGRITY

A person who uses their authority to meet the goals and objectives of a mission for the sake of the victim or their crew is demonstrating true integrity. Integrity is not based on one's own personal or private gain. It also entails truthfulness to your supervisor and your crew. Integrity can be shared with your crew by encouraging open and honest communications.

JUDGMENT

Judgment is a trait that presents accountability to a leader's actions. A leader who demonstrates good, sound judgment always considers a range of alternatives before making a final decision. This same leader will think out the possible effects, whether detrimental or benficial, of decisions before they are made.

JUSTICE

As indicated above, a good leader will think about the decision about to be made. In thinking of this, he will make this decision based on supporting the mission goals and taking into account the needs of the crew members. Listen to all sides of an issue before making a decision that affects your crew. Recognize the need to be consistent in applying praise and criticism to your crew.

KNOWLEDGE

A good leader has the capability to make sound judgment calls and tactical decisions. In addition, he is able not only to perform operational tasks well, but is proficient in administrative matters. The leader is knowledgeable in what should be done and when. He recognizes, then corrects inadequate performance by a crew member. The best way to ensure your crew is knowledgeable is by setting the example yourself.

TACT

Respect and tact are synonymous. A tactful leader is respectful when speaking with his subordinates and supervisor. Tactfulness is necessary when operating in the public's view or anywhere your actions will be perceived as representing the entire organization.

LOYALTY

To be a professional leader is to accept your assignment, however difficult or adverse, without expressing your personal criticism. Loyalty to your crew means you will stand up for them against unfair treatment from others or from your supervisors. Loyalty within the crew is accomplished by encouraging open discussions of problems in the unit and individually with your crew members. Remember keep confidential matters between you and the confiding crew member.

SELFLESSNESS

It is not a luxury to be a crewleader. It is a sacrifice. Your responsibilities begin with your assignment and then continue to your crew members. Ensure that the needs of your subordinates are met before attending to your own needs. A good leader takes whatever actions are necessary to provide for the welfare of each crew member. As a crew, you share the hardships, dangers and discomforts with them.

PRINCIPLES OF LEADERSHIP

There are 11 basic principles of leadership that a good leader will strive to meet in developing an effective leadership role. These principles are basic guidelines for what crewleaders should do. They are not to be construed as guidelines on how to lead; that will be discussed in the next section. These 11 principles are straightforward, simplistic, and apply throughout all levels of leadership and can carry-over into your personal life. Many of these cover your own self-improvement as well as how you treat others.

SELF-IMPROVEMENT, SELF-REALIZATION

Look around at the leaders in your life, whether they are friends, other searchers or fellow employees. What is it about them that makes them a good leader? Search out good leaders and compare the traits you see in them to make an honest assessment of yourself. Ask other leaders what they see in you and what improvements or changes they recommend.

BE KNOWLEDGEABLE AND TACTICALLY EFFICIENT

Know your job and know it well. Do your job and do it well. Sounds easy right? It is essentially impossible to gain the respect and confidence of the people you will lead unless you are fully knowledgeable and capable of performing the tasks you will be asking them to do. Gaining your crew's respect will have them turning to you for advice and guidance in completing your objectives.

SEEK RESPONSIBILITY AND TAKE RESPONSIBILITY

When you see that something needs to be done, do it. Do not wait until someone tells you to do it. In taking responsibility, you should realize two aspects: be responsible when something goes wrong on your crew, when something goes right, freely pass the praise to everyone. Take the pain. Share the pleasure.

MAKE SOUND AND TIMELY DECISIONS

A mediocre decision made on time beats a good decision made too late. Time versus quality of the decision is what should be weighed in making a good choice. There are several steps to consider and these steps appear in every decision someone makes, whether consciously or subconsciously. First you need to define the problem. This means defining both the symptoms and the cause. Get the true problem clear in your mind before trying to act on it. Next, you need to analyze and get all the facts. Effectively clarifying the problem and solutions will determine the direction of the decision. You will need to determine what the alternatives are. The leader must weigh the time spent gathering information against the urgency of the decision. Once the alternatives are established, the leader will need to test them mentally and begin the process of elimination to determine which is the best course of action. The leader now takes the best solution available at the moment and implements it; or puts the decision into action. The leader will always take the effort to follow-up his decision, and critique his decisions; taking input from his subordinates and fellow leaders. The above decision making procedure appears to be a long, complex process not suited to the world of emergency response. Decisions made using this format occur quickly. A good decision maker may not even realize these steps were followed. The good leader can quickly sum up a situation, consider the options, choose and implement the action and follow-up the results in order to learn from what has happened.

SET THE EXAMPLE

There is no motivation better than leading by example. It is by far the best inspiration to your crew members to "Work with me and do as I do" than just "Do it because I say so." If you, as a leader, expect your subordinates to do the

Chapter 2 - Small Unit Leadership

work, then be prepared to do it yourself.

CARE ABOUT THE PEOPLE YOU LEAD

A good leader cares for and tries to understand the needs and wants of the people he supervises. Your crew members are individual people with purposes of their own that do not necessarily coincide with your or the organization views.

SHARE INFORMATION

Your crew members are involved in the mission and have as much at stake trying to meet your objectives as you have meeting the goals given to you as a crewleader. Keep your crew members informed whenever you have the time. You will save time explaining now instead of being asked questions during critical situations.

CREATE RESPONSIBILITY IN YOUR CREW MEMBERS

Once you have discovered your crew members have the skill and desire to do the work, then let them do it. A good leader recognizes ability in crew members and delegates assignments appropriately. Let your subordinates work on tasks with the understanding that, along with the authority to do the job, they have the responsibility to you to complete the task correctly.

TASK ORIENTATION: INSTRUCT, SUPERVISE AND SUPPORT

A leader should distribute tasks among his crew members. Ensure the tasks are explained in detail and the members know what to do and how to accomplish them. Check the crew member's performance from time to time to ensure two things: that your crew member knows you are there to help them, and that you are responsible for the task being completed correctly.

CREATE A TEAM

Building trust between a leader and the crew is important, but developing trust between crew members is what helps make your unit a team. Crew members need to have confidence in their abilities while having confidence in the abilities of the other crew members. Crew members need to be aware of how their own individual performances affect other members and the overall mission.

MATCH THE CREW TO THE ASSIGNMENT

Leaders know what their subordinates need to do to complete an assignment. Good leaders know what they can do. Make sure that the level of performance needed to complete a certain assignment is not too far beyond the skills of your crew. Remember, your total crew work output is no stronger than its weakest member. Do not make the assignment too easy; it will not challenge your crew members. A good stretch of abilities will make better crew members for future assignments.

LEADERSHIP PROCEDURES

In a search and rescue mission, the crewleader has defined responsibilities. These responsibilities are an essential part of the entire operation. As a Crew/Strike Team/Task Force leader you report to a Division/Group Supervisor. From this supervisor you will be assigned tactical assignments in which it is your responsibility to report progress, resource status, and other information. It is your responsibility to maintain required records on your assignment and assigned personnel.

There are 6 tasks required of a Crew/Strike Team/Task Force Leader in the NIIMS Field Operation Guide (ICS-420-1):

1. **Review Common Responsibilities;**

    a. Receive assignments,

    b. Check in at designated location,

    c. Receive briefing from immediate supervisor,

    d. Acquire work materials,

e. Organize and brief subordinates,

f. Use clear text/ICS terminology in all radio communications,

g. Complete required forms and reports,

h. Respond to demobilization orders and brief subordinates of same.

2. **Review assignments with subordinates and assign tasks;**

3. **Monitor work progress and make changes when necessary;**

4. **Coordinate activities with adjacent Strike Team/Task Force and single resources;**

5. **Travel to and from active assignment area with assigned resources;**

6. **Retain control of resources while in "Available" or "Out-of-Service" status.**

MANAGEMENT THEORIES AND TECHNIQUES

Managing people, either as individuals or as a combined unit requires different approaches based upon your situation. There are four categories of managing techniques discussed below that, when used together, will make accomplishing your mission easier.

CONFLICT MANAGEMENT

Conflict management is considered an out dated form of management. It is an approach based on reaction instead of pro-action. Changes in policy, procedure, or objectives are made after a conflict arises.

Much of the conflict management style can be traced back to the authoritarian military style of management and management practices utilized during and after the Industrial Revolution to control unskilled labor. Proponents of conflict management believe it is necessary to reach their objectives in this manner to gain as much production as possible from the workforce. This form of management is task-oriented, with little or no preplanning or attention to employee needs.

SITUATIONAL MANAGEMENT

This style of management is simple. You are given a situation, or in our term, a mission to complete. Utilizing a flexible approach, you can implement a plan that will best serve the organization, your crew members, and accomplish the mission in the most effective and efficient manner.

Briefly stated, the leader adapts his management style to his followers. While a particular style of management may be extremely effective in one situation, it can have disastrous effects in another.

Even though a leader's basic management style is important, it is equally important for a good leader to adjust that style according to the circumstances that exist. This is situational leadership.

SUPERVISORY TECHNIQUES

A good leader is knowledgeable and efficient in the tasks required to complete the mission. A great leader gets the work done through the efforts of others. This is supervision.

For a leader to successfully be able to supervise, he must have the leadership traits and practice the leadership principles discussed earlier. The 8 basic elements of successful supervision are listed:

1. Communication

As a leader, you need to take the time to listen to your crew members; keeping them informed in the process. When you receive new information or orders, get the word to them when practical. Successful communication is a two-way street. Encourage your subordinates to be open and hon-

Chapter 2 - Small Unit Leadership

est with you in their discussions. Never belittle a crew member for delivering bad news.

2. Teamwork

Establish from the beginning that all of you are a team. Coordinate the tactics used to complete the mission so that crew members depend on each other. A good leader actively solicits input from the crew members. This helps to keep subordinates interested in what is going on.

3. Involvement

Not only does a leader desire honest input from subordinates, but uses this input and makes changes based on their suggestions. Leaders should provide crew members opportunities to use their skills to the fullest in completing the mission.

4. Initiative

A leader should always demonstrate initiative and encourage it from subordinates. If you have a crew member who wishes to take that extra effort in reaching the mission goals, then allow the freedom to do so. Leaders should expect the crew member's work to be up to standards and completed within time. A good leader will use mistakes as a positive learning experience and work with the crew to determine what the best approach should have been.

5. Positive Supervision

A leader should care about the wants and needs of his subordinates and help provide for these when necessary. There is probably no better motivator than a leader that stands by the actions of subordinates and recognizes crew members for good performance.

6. Set Standards

The leader sets the pace... No better phrase can sum up the value of setting good standards for subordinates to follow. A good leader needs to establish standards that are challenging, but not impossible. Use the input of subordinates in setting these standards and timetables. When your mission is complete, use these standards to critique you and your crew's performance.

7. Control Measures

The basic control measures issued to a leader is the mission assignment. It contains the parameters of the mission and the desired actions requested by the organization. Within the crew, a leader can establish control measures based on the resources assigned to him and their qualifications. The key to establishing control measures is to keep them measurable and realistic. A good leader is able to adjust these control measures when he observes substandard performance.

8. Performance Feedback

Your crew or team needs feedback on how they are performing. Both good and bad progress needs to be communicated to them in order for corrections to be made. Leaders need to coach individual subordinates to improve their performance. If you, as a leader, are doing your job right, then your crew members will want to do their job correctly. Use the standards you and your subordinates established to evaluate your progress.

MOTIVATIONAL TECHNIQUES

Everyone has wants and needs that effect what they do and how well they do it. These wants and needs have been broken down into a hierarchy by psychologists and sociologists into 5 categories: Physiological, Security, Social Acceptance, Ego and Self-fulfillment. Studies by behavioral science researchers have discovered the physiological and safety needs, although important, are less important to subordinates when compared with social acceptance as part of a group and prestige as part of a group recognized by others. In other words, these studies show people will work for less in order to satisfy their ego and self-fulfillment needs.

A conscientious leader pays close attention to a subordinate's basic needs—food, clothing, shelter, but also needs to listen to them and discover what is important to them. You can take what is important to your crew members and relate to them how achieving the mission will satisfy these needs.

Below are listed some examples of motivators, as well as demotivators that can effect the overall performance of your crew.

Motivators

1. Care about your subordinates;

2. Be aware of your own biases and prejudices;

3. Give praise when appropriate;

4. Take responsibility for others;

5. Build independence;

6. Exhibit personal diligence;

7. Be willing to learn from others;

8. Demonstrate confidence;

9. Encourage ingenuity;

10. Delegate, Delegate, Delegate.

Demotivators

1. Never belittle a subordinate;

2. Never criticize a subordinate in front of others;

3. Never play favorites;

4. Never take all the credit, share it with your crew;

5. Never lower your personal standards;

6. Never fail to help your subordinates grow; fight for them.

Conclusion

Sound leadership knowledge and practices are critical to the successful completion of your goals and objectives. Dynamic leadership can lead to performance that is positive, highly successful and innovative.

To restate an old adage, "Leaders are not born, they are made." Good leaders are born of their own efforts. Someone has placed you in this role of responsibility and given you the task of developing your leadership skills and practices to support both the goals of the organization and the people you will lead.

Chapter 2 - Small Unit Leadership

REVIEW QUESTIONS

1. List at least five of the sixteen Leadership Traits for small unit leaders.

   _____   _____
   _____   _____
   _____

2. List at least six of the eleven Principles of Leadership.

   _____   _____
   _____   _____
   _____   _____

3. Reviewing common responsibilities, reviewing assigments and monitoring work progress are all part of the tasks outlined in the?

   _____

4. _____ Management is considered out-dated, designed for inexperience and untrained personnel, and task oriented.

5. _____ Management is considered flexible and adaptable.

6. List at least six of the eight supervisory techniques.

   _____   _____
   _____   _____
   _____   _____

7. _____ and _____ have been determined by social scientists to be the most important in satisfying the wants and needs of personnel.

8. List five motivators.

   _____   _____
   _____   _____
   _____

9. List five demotivators.

   _____   _____
   _____   _____
   _____

10. One who is charged with the responsibility of accomplishing an assignment through the efforts of others is a definition of? _____

NOTES:

FITNESS FOR THE CREWLEADER

OBJECTIVES

A. The student shall explain the techniques used to physically prepare for a SAR response.

B. The student shall describe the relationship between physical ability and the mental aspects of effective search techniques.

C. The student shall describe a basic understanding of nutritional needs during extended periods of physical exertion.

FITNESS FOR THE CREWLEADER

This chapter is designed to continue on the building blocks that were developed during the FUNSAR/SAR TECH™ II material contained in Search and Rescue Fundamentals.

The tasks that are expected of a SAR TECH™ I /Crewleader III are by definition both physically and mentally challenging. A team leader must maintain good physical and mental conditioning at all times. The Crewleader must also have a good working knowledge of physical and mental conditioning so that they can recognize problems that may arise with members of their team while on a search.

You must be able to take care of yourself before you can take care of others.

FITNESS

A Crewleader must maintain good physical and mental conditioning at all times to be prepared to operate under the conditions encountered on searches. Crewleaders that are physically fit will be better prepared to face survival or rescue incidents than those that are not.

For these reasons, this chapter will look at the basics of physical and mental conditioning as it pertains to the SAR TECH™ I/Crewleader III. This information is only the tip of the iceberg on mental and physical conditioning.

Search and Rescue involves a number of diverse variables that can, and do, directly or indirectly affect the Search and Rescue Crewleader and member. The areas that can affect any SAR TECH™ are:

1) **Extremes in temperature**
2) **Lack of proper rest-work cycles**
3) **Availability of water**
4) **Availability of food (proper diet)**
5) **The potential for a rescue turned survival situation.**

Prior to starting any physical conditioning program, consult a medical doctor and explain to him/her the physical conditioning program on which you are about to partake. Also explain and describe the rigors of working in the Search and Rescue environment.

Physical conditioning is generally broken down into four basic areas. These areas can be identified as Strength, Agility, Flexibility and Endurance.

STRENGTH

The requirement of physical strength for a SAR TECHänician should be obvious. A SAR TECHä I must be capable of carrying the required equipment over hazardous terrain in bad weather and be capable of staying focused on the mission. If personnel are lacking in physical strength, all aspects of the searches will be affected. The person who is focused on the weight of the pack or the pain in the legs from walking is not focused on the search objective(s).

AGILITY

Agility is the ability to quickly alter or change the direction of travel or course with speed and in a fluid manner. Agility is as important a component of a workout as Strength, Flexibility and Endurance.

FLEXIBILITY

Physical strength goes hand-in-hand with flexibility. If someone is physically strong but can not move freely due to body bulk, then the physical strength is wasted because it cannot be used effectively.

ENDURANCE

The fourth area is endurance. Endurance requires the body to be capable of keeping oxygenated blood flowing to the entire body. This includes the brain for logic and making good decisions. The muscles need a steady supply in order to continue to walk, climb, run or perform other required physical activities.

Chapter 3 - Fitness For The Crew Leader

PHYSICAL CONDITIONING WORKOUTS

A good workout or physical conditioning routine should encompass physical training that includes strength building exercises, flexibility exercises and endurance ability.

STRENGTH BUILDING

Strength building can be accomplished by several exercises, some of which are lifting weights, push ups, and pull ups. When working with weights, ensure that there is a safety spotter at all times. Start out with a light weight and work up in repetitions before starting to add weight. The idea is to get a good mix between repetitions and weight. A good rule of thumb is to be able to bench press your body weight. This ensures that a person can at least handle their own body weight in an emergency situation. The most common mistake made is pushing the weight limit too fast and thus causing injury. The second most common mistake is not using a spotter and, in turn, becoming injured.

FLEXIBILITY TRAINING

Flexibility training should consist of exercises that assist in stretching. Some of the more common exercises are windmills, arm twirls, trunk twists and four step mountain climbers. The common purpose of each exercise is to stretch out the tendons and muscles.

Start slowly to allow the body to warm up. Be systematic in stretching. Warm up and stretch all of the parts of the body i.e. neck, shoulders, back, hips, legs, ankles, etc. One of the best ways to stretch is to start at the top (neck) and work down (ankles).

But, remember, stretching should not be forced. Do not use jerky motions. You do not want to tear anything; you want to stretch it. Also you should always stretch before and after strength or endurance workouts.

ENDURANCE TRAINING

Endurance training is the third part to the conditioning triangle. Endurance allows the Crewleader/Member to make use of the strength and flexibility over a longer period of time. A member that quickly tires out and has to stop is the weak link on the team and thus holds the team back from the mission goal, finding the victim.

The simplest and most common endurance training exercises are running, bicycling and cross country skiing machines. At one time, running was considered the ultimate aerobic exercise. Running can cause problems with the joints of the body, especially the knees, ankles and hips. A person that is over their target weight is adding extra stress to the joints every time the foot strikes the ground while running. Bicycle riding and cross country ski machines remove the harsh impacts on the body that are introduced with running. As with each of the above exercises, care should be given when warming up, cooling down and setting repetition schedules. Start low and work up slowly. Warm up prior to working out and warm down after the work out.

MENTAL CONDITIONING

Mental conditioning is as important as physical. One of the easiest forms of mental conditioning is training. If a person encounters stressful situations while in training, they will be better equipped to deal with it when it occurs during a search. Being mentally prepared for Search and Rescue situations also includes thinking through situations before they occur. This can and should include talking through the procedures to be handled while enroute to an incident site or crash site. By talking through the procedures (check lists are very good here), a Crewleader will already have created a "mental picture" of what the Team will be doing on the scene.

MENTAL FATIGUE

The other side of mental conditioning is mental fatigue. When working a search operation, it is not uncommon to work long hours, eat poor quality and/or little food and have little or no sleep. Mental fatigue can be recognized by irritability, lack of patience and lack of or poor judgment or decision making.

This is a very important area where crewleaders need to watch their crew members.

By observing the crew, a leader can stop a problem before it occurs. One very important part of the search base equipment should be a book or some form of music. It creates a mental escape for the crew member/leader. Even if it is only for 30 minutes, it mentally and emotionally takes the team leader/member out of the stressful environment of a search operation.

Proper sleep and diet are also very important to mental health and conditioning. A crewleader should ensure that all members get proper sleep on their off shift hours. Crews should not be allowed to work more than a single 12 hour rotation and should have mandated down time to allow them to mentally and physically recuperate.

Many times SAR personnel tend to get the "superman" syndrome thinking they can go on and on and on. This leads to accidents and could contribute to deaths. A good crewleader will ensure that their crew gets enough sleep. This problem also extends to all support positions on a search; especially base operations personnel that forget that mental work many times is as hard, if not harder, than physical work on a search.

In some extreme situations, people may be asked to extend their shifts past a twelve hour rotation. As a Crewleader, you must assess the physical and mental condition of your crew to determine if they can continue within the limits of the risk / benefit factor.

The best solution for the problem of mental fatigue is to mentally escape from the environment (book, music, etc.) and to get proper sleep. An overtired searcher is not an alert searcher and does nobody any good on a search, especially the victim for whom we are looking.

Mental fatigue can lead to numerous problems while in the field on a SAR team. A healthy mental attitude includes the ability to realize physical limitations.

Everyone is affected by weather extremes of heat, cold and the wind. If a searcher is overtired and not thinking properly, he/she will have a tendency to push beyond normal limitations and enter into some serious safety problems. Any member of the crew, especially the crewleader, should feel comfortable in calling for a rest break. It is the job of the crewleader to monitor his/her people and be able to determine when mental or physical breaks are required.

Progress and the pace of the crew should be geared to the slowest and or weakest member of the crew. There is no disgrace in having to slow down for a member but there is for allowing a crew member to get hurt or killed because the crew's speed forced a weaker member to push beyond his/her limits and becomes hurt.

An excellent mental attitude will help a crewleader/member overcome any physical or mental obstacle that occurs on a search. A Crewleader must know his/her own limitations and the limitations of their crew members.

NUTRITIONAL REQUIREMENTS

Preplanning for nutritional requirements on a search needs to start before the search. Plan for a well balanced diet designed to fulfill the nutritional needs of the search. The food supply should be designed using 3700 calories a day as an average requirement for search and rescue workers during a search.

There are three categories of food to be examined. They are:

1) **Fats**

2) **Carbohydrates**

3) **Proteins**

FATS

Fats contain energy that is burned at a slower rate than those contained in carbohydrates. Because of this, the fats are a longer lasting form of energy than carbohydrates. Fats also supply certain vitamins that are water soluble. A few examples of fats are margarine, egg yolks, oils, nuts, cheese and butter.

CARBOHYDRATES

Carbohydrates consist of very simple molecules. They are easily digested and lose little of their energy during this process. They are efficient suppliers of energy. Some examples of carbohydrates are sugars, starches and cellulose.

These can be found in vegetables, candy, cereals, baked goods, rice, pasta and fruits.

PROTEIN

Protein is broken down during the digestive process into various amino acids. Body tissue such as muscles are formed by these amino acids. Protein that lacks one or more of these essential amino acids are referred to as "incomplete". Proteins that provide the body with the exact amino acids required to rebuild itself are called "complete". Some complete protein is found in fish, meat and poultry.

When amino acids are introduced into the body in large quantities and all are not used for the rebuilding of muscles, they are stored in the body as fat or burned as fuel. Because protein has the most complex molecules of the three (carbohydrate, fats and protein), it is used to supply energy after the other forms of energy have been used up.

SUMMARY

The better you are physically and mentally conditioned before you are called to a search, the better you will be able to lead...and search. A properly conditioned SAR worker is also less likely to suffer from severe fatigue.

REVIEW QUESTIONS

1. List the four parts of a physical fitness program.
   _____   _____
   _____   _____

2. The recommended caloric intake for working individuals on a SAR mission is?
   _____

3. Foods to be consumed during missions should include:
   _____   _____
   _____

4. Using checklists is a good way to help increase _____ conditioning.

5. _____ before beginning any fitness program.

6. The use of books, games, music, etc are important outlets for searchers combating?
   _____

NOTES:

Chapter 4 - Crew Safety

CREW SAFETY

OBJECTIVES

A. The student shall be able to identify and describe the six (6) special hazards encountered on a SAR mission.

1. Climatic hazards

2. Forest fires

3. Hunters/poachers

4. Searching on private property

5. Drug production areas

6. Animals

CREW SAFETY

As a Crewleader it is your responsibility to assure that you and/or your crew do not become "part of the incident".

A. Maintain the attitude that everyone on your crew has a "round trip ticket", and, everyone is coming back from the mission.

B. Pre-plan with your crew as to what your evacuation plans will be in the event that:
1. The weather deteriorates
2. Someone is injured
3. Conditions become too hazardous to continue the assigned mission.

C. Pre-plan with the Incident Command Post as to what your evacuation plan will be.

D. Make certain that you know where all your crew members are located in your assigned area.

E. Make certain that the Incident Command Post is aware of your crew's location and check in regularly.

CLIMATIC HAZARDS

Obviously, we cannot plan for all of our search missions to be conducted in fair weather! The fact is that "weather conditions" may be the very reason that we are out searching for the subject in the first place.

It would be difficult to plan for all types of weather prior to entering the field, but a few considerations should be made in your planning.

A. Be familiar with the usual weather patterns in your part of the country, and, plan accordingly. Are regular afternoon thunder storms likely? Or, regular snow storms?

B. What special weather conditions are imminent? Is there a cold (or warm) front on the horizon?

It will be your responsibility to assure that your crew is generally prepared for the climatic conditions you are likely to encounter. Your crew will only be as "strong as its weakest link." Don't let the weather make matters worse. Before you set out on your mission:

1. Do a "pack check" to assure that all members of your crew have clothing that will be adequate for the expected conditions. If a crew member lacks something, try to provide what will be needed, or don't let them go out.

2. Obtain the latest weather reports for the area.

3. Pre-plan with your crew and the ICP what your course of action will be if the weather deteriorates to the point that continuing your assigned mission will be too hazardous for your assigned personnel.

SPECIAL CONSIDERATIONS:

Thunderstorms

Thunderstorms pose a special and deadly threat aside from the obvious lightning hazard. These storms develop rapidly, appear suddenly and move through the area relatively quickly. They are capable of doing significant damage from the winds they generate. Further, tornado activity is likely to be spawned by the storm, adding to the hazard.

1. **Micro-bursts:** This is a common phenomenon associated with thunderstorms. Generally thought to be a tornado within the storm, a micro-burst is a high speed down draft of cold air. A micro-burst is characterized by damage that appears to be caused by the wind moving in one direction only, i.e.:

Chapter 4 - Crew Safety

trees broken off, lined up parallel to each other, and all pointing in one direction.

2. **Hail**: This is caused by rain drops that have formed within the storm which are then caught up in the air currents before becoming heavy enough to fall to the ground. The winds within the storm move in all directions, carrying the rain drops with them. When the rain is carried high enough it freezes and forms an ice pellet. When the ice pellet falls, it gathers a layer of water from its surroundings. If it now is carried aloft again, the water freezes forming another layer of ice over the first. When it falls again, more water is added. Should this ice pellet continue to "cycle" through the storm, more and more layers of ice will be added until it becomes too heavy for the process to continue, or until it is caught up in a micro-burst.

3. **Lightning**: This is caused by electrical discharges between a cloud and the ground, or between two or more clouds. Millions of volts of electricity may be discharged in each lightning bolt. Generally speaking, all electricity will "seek ground". When the cloud is "charged" with an electrical potential (positive or negative) and the ground is charged with the opposite (relative to the cloud) potential (again, either positive or negative) the two charges are attracted and an arc is formed to discharge the difference in potentials - a lightning bolt.

4. **Rain**: Significant amounts of rain may fall during the thunderstorm in a relatively short period of time. Up to several inches in a matter of 1-2 hours is not uncommon. This may create additional hazards in areas due to the "runoff" of the water —flash flooding.

What should you do as the Crewleader when faced with a thunderstorm? Get yourself and your crew out of the area as quickly as possible! In the interim - seek shelter. There will be little you can do in the event of tornadoes, microbursts and hail. **For lightning:**

1. Seek a vegetated area that is relatively uniform in height. Electricity will "seek the path of least resistance" and the air represents resistance. The lightning bolt will (generally) discharge to the tallest object in the area. Avoid the tallest objects, and, don't become one yourself.

2. Avoid pine trees. Most pine trees have large tap roots that seek the water table in the ground. They can act as "living lightning rods".

3. Discard any metal objects that you might be carrying, i.e.: tent poles, walking sticks, etc.

4. Seek shelter in a building that is well grounded.

5. Seek shelter in a vehicle. This is probably the safest place that you can be. Should lightning strike a vehicle, the charge will travel on the very outside of the vehicle and into the ground.

6. Stay dry. Your body will lose heat 25 times faster to water than it will to air. The rain from a thunderstorm is colder than any other type of rain.

7. Avoid low lying areas where water will collect from the runoff of the rain. Remember significant amounts of rain will be falling in a relatively short period of time.

Cold Weather

Cold weather presents a special hazard that may take a period of time to become apparent. There are three specific hazards associated with the cold weather:

1. **Hypothermia** (low body temperature) is caused by the loss of body heat to its surroundings. This may be due to convection (wind, or in water), radiation (lack of sufficient shell layer), conduction (laying against the cold ground), respiration (heavy breathing while exerting), and perspiration (sweating). It is characterized by:

    A. Uncontrollable shivering
    B. Loss of rational thinking
    C. Loss of motor control (unsteady gait and jerky movements)
    D. Listlessness
    E. Numbness
    F. Slowed respiration
    G. Slowed pulse rate

2. **Frost Nip** is the early stages of Frost Bite and occurs locally to exposed flesh. Characterized by:
    A. Pain in the effected area(s).
    B. Swelling in the effected area(s).
    C. Redness in the effected area(s).

3. **Frost Bite** is when exposed flesh freezes and ice crystals form in the skin. It is characterized by:
    A. Loss of sensation in the effected area(s).
    B. A "whitish" or "grayish" appearance of the effected area(s).
    C. The area(s) will be rigid to the touch.

As the Crewleader, assure that all of your crew is prepared to be out in the cold weather with the proper use of "layering". Specifically:

1. Everyone should have, and know how to use, all four layers of clothing - underwear, clothing, insulation, and shell. Assure that everyone has (and uses) gloves and hats. 80% of the body's heat loss is out of the top of the head. Generally, if your hands or feet are cold - put on your hat!

2. Assess your crew members regularly to assure that they are staying warm. One of the first signs of hypothermia is the loss of the ability to think rationally. If one of your crew becomes hypothermic, stop immediately and warm that individual.

3. Fluid replacement will be of critical importance, even in cold environments due to the body losing water because of the reduced humidity in the air. Assure that everyone is consuming plenty of water (see below).

Warming individuals that are affected, either locally (Frost Nip or Frost Bite) or systematically (Hypothermic) should be done slowly and evenly. More damage can be caused by warming the individual too rapidly, particularly in the case of Frost Bite. It will be important to assure that a "layering" of temperatures is avoided. When a person is chilled (from the elements), in effect, their internal temperature will still be higher than the area(s) that have been chilled. If the area(s) are now heated, a "layering" of temperatures can occur. Specifically: internally the tissue is one temperature, then a layer of colder tissue, then a layer of warmer tissue caused by the warming. This will cause more extensive damage to already damaged tissue, and will make that tissue more susceptible to future cooling.

Generally:

1. Remove the individual from the elements to as warm a place as possible.

2. Attempt to warm the individual [or the area(s) effected] from within, i.e. with warmed drinks containing sugar.

3. If you do add heat, i.e. warm water, make certain that the water is not so hot that it will scald the effected area(s). The water should be no hotter than 103 to 104 degrees (warm to the touch).

4. Once the individuals are affected by the cold, they must be removed from the search as they will be more susceptible to the effects of the cold later on.

Hot Weather

Hot weather is just as hazardous as cold weather. Under exertion, your body will produce heat which must be dissipated. Generally, this is accomplished by sweating. In order to sweat the body must have sufficient water to form the sweat. When you sweat, you lose electrolytes (salts and minerals) that will need to be replaced. There are several electrolyte solutions that are available commercially that are designed to replace fluids and electrolytes lost due to sweating. Among these are Gatorade, Powerade, and the like. These are formulated to replace fluids. Evidence suggests that using these drinks while still active may cause water requirements to increase (these drinks contain a large amount of simple sugar in the form of simple carbohydrates - where carbohydrate goes, so does water). In general, the best plan is to consume water while exerting, then, replace the electrolytes you have lost with one of these formulas during recovery (after you are out of the field). Drinking the formula while exerting may make matters worse!

Specific hot weather hazards:

1. **Heat Cramps** are caused by a loss of electrolytes due to sweating, particularly potassium. As the body losses potassium the muscles are unable to relax after they have been contracted, causing a cramp. When this occurs, stop and replace the potassium. The best plan is to avoid the situation in the first place. Carry foods rich in potassium (like a banana) with you in the field.

2. **Heat Exhaustion** is caused by the same process as Heat Cramps, but the effect is more systemic. In some areas the term "Bear Caught" is used to describe Heat Exhaustion. It is characterized by:
    Listlessness
    Nausea
    Vomiting
    Weakness
    Profuse sweating
    Pallor
Again avoid the situation as you would for Heat Cramps. If Heat Exhaustion does occur:
   • Stop immediately and cool the individual down.
   • Replace the fluids with water (now use the electrolyte formula).
   • Remove the individual to base camp.

3. **Heat Stroke** is the most deadly of the three. It is caused by a break down of the body's sweating mechanism due, in part, to lack of fluids. When the sweating mechanism breaks down and the individual stops sweating, the body temperature rises quickly. When the

body temperature rises above a certain point (usually 104 to 105 degrees [F]) brain death begins to occur. Body temperatures above 108 degrees [F] are not uncommon in cases of Heat Stroke. This is a true medical emergency and needs to be addressed rapidly. Heat Stroke is characterized by:

> Rapid onset of symptoms.
> Flushed appearance (bright red skin)
> NO sweating
> Hot (to the touch) skin.
> Unconsciousness
> Seizure activity

If a Heat Stroke should occur:
- Stop immediately and render aid.
- Cool the individual as rapidly as possible. Remove their clothing and flood them with cool water.
- If possible, submerge them in the water, using care that they don't drown.
- Don't give them anything by mouth. Most everything will come back up when (or if) a seizure occurs. Vomiting will create an airway problem.
- Call for evacuation immediately.

Some have thought that rapid cooling of the individual may bring on seizures. The seizures will occur anyway and with them, brain death. The individual's best chance for survival is to have their body temperature returned to normal as quickly as possible. They can't do it on their own, so you have to do it for them!

As a rule, in hot weather:

1. Assure that everyone on your crew has at least two liters of water. It is generally held that water requirements are: one gallon of water per person per day, more if the individual is exerting. Water requirements rise dramatically in hot environments and consumption should rise with it.

2. Stop to rest frequently and assure that everyone is drinking water. If you wait until you feel thirsty, you have already reached the point that fluid replacement is of importance.

3. In general, a well hydrated person will produce 30 to 50 cc's of urine per hour. When the bladder contains 300 to 350 cc's of urine, the individual will feel the need to void. A good "rule of thumb" might be that everyone on you crew should void at least twice during a 12 hour Operations period.

FOREST FIRES

Forest fires present a special hazard to search crews and the best philosophy is to evacuate the area as quickly as possible. Crewleaders should

maintain contact with the Incident Command Post for reports of fires in your area. Forest and Wildland fires can become major conflagrations in a very short period of time, trapping and killing everything in their wakes. Large Wildland fires can become "fire storms" very rapidly when the conditions become favorable for the fire!

SPECIAL CONSIDERATIONS:

Fire Storm: A "fire storm" occurs when the conflagration grows to the point that it will create its own weather patterns. This situation can become virtually impossible to control.

Crowning: When the fire is fanned by wind and reaches temperatures that burns green vegetation, the fire will move into the tops of the trees. When this occurs the fire will move rapidly through the crowns of the trees, and, in some cases, will not burn the underlying vegetation.

Chapter 4 - Crew Safety

In general, the best plan is to vacate the area, specifically:
1. Keep the ICP updated on your location so that you can be evacuated as quickly as possible.

2. Should a fire be reported in your area, if possible, move your crew upwind of the reported location of the fire.

3. Know the prevailing wind patterns in your assigned area, i.e.: in the mountains, the air will move up-slope during the day and down-slope during the night.

HUNTERS/POACHERS

Not all the hazards encountered by SAR crews and SAR Crewleaders are natural. Many can be man made or humans themselves. In many cases, the hazards encountered are not intentional. The best way to safeguard the SAR crew members is to be aware of these potential dangers.

Hunters

In most cases hunters would not deliberately pose a hazard or hindrance to SAR workers. They are concerned with their hunt and the taking of game. However, there are several risks that hunters can pose for the SAR crews.

Hunters tend to become fixated on their hunt and often will not be as aware of their surroundings and environment as they should be. This can include their awareness that there are, in fact, SAR crews in their immediate area.

Hunters who are fixated on their pursuit may tend to become hostile or aggressive if SAR workers inadvertently surprise them. If SAR crews are perceived to have startled or scared away the game that the hunters are pursuing, that may be cause for aggression as well.

There is also the possibility that some hunters will fire on an unknown target believing that it is game. Further, there is the possibility that a hunter may believe that the SAR workers are trespassers or poachers and may become hostile to them.

Hunters most often will hunt with firearms, either modern or black powder, but may also use bow and arrow. While most hunters will attempt to use caution and consideration when hunting, there are, unfortunately, those cases where hunters do not always exercise the best of judgment.

The SAR workers, and especially Crewleaders, should be aware that anytime they are in or around hunters, there is the potential for a mishap. If a SAR crew should encounter hunters who are using their firearms or other hunting equipment in an unsafe manner, the crew should take steps to leave the area. They should also notify the Incident Command staff of this hazard so that other crews that may be sent into the area can be diverted around it or can be forewarned. If necessary, the appropriate law enforcement agency should be notified.

General Safeguards:

There are a number of steps which SAR workers and Crewleaders can take to help alleviate or minimize the threats posed by hunters.

The first, and most basic, is to be aware of the hunting season in progress in the search areas. If you know that you are going to be searching in a prime hunting area during one of the various hunting seasons, you know that your awareness has to be heightened for associated hazards.

Another basic safeguard is to wear bright, easily seen clothing. Blaze or International orange is one of the more accepted colors for ready identification. It should be kept in mind, however, that, during the fall season in various areas of the country, the changing and falling leaves will take on an orange color. This could tend to cause the SAR worker to blend into the surroundings. Therefore, the potential would still be there for a hunter who sees movement to fire without getting a positive identification.

As with all searching, the crew members and Crewleaders need to constantly be aware of their surroundings and environment. This includes knowing whether you are searching in a hunting area and whether or not there is a potential for hunters to be in the region. You can ordinarily avoid many of the dangers when encountering hunters by making your presence known as you progress through your search area; by not concealing yourself within heavy brush; and by using basic common sense techniques.

Poachers

Unlike seasonal licensed hunters, poachers pose a unique and much more dangerous threat to SAR crews. Poachers are engaged in a criminal activity for which they do not wish to be caught. This will cause some to take extreme and drastic measures to avoid being detected and apprehended.

Poachers quite often have a criminal past and know that if they are caught, arrested and convicted, they will receive a heavy fine and/or jail time. Due to this, poachers have been known to take violent action when discovered by any intruders.

SAR crews may be mistaken by poachers as being government employees, i.e. game wardens or other law enforcement officials.

Extreme caution should be utilized anytime you are working in an area where there is the potential for poachers to be active.

There are several different methods of poaching. There are snare traps and dead fall traps which poachers will use to entrap game. They also use firearms and sometimes, bow and arrow.

Poachers, due to their backgrounds, often do not take the time to identify their targets. Further their various types of traps can ensnare or seriously injure a human as well as the animals for which they were intended.

It should also be remembered that poachers often will engage in drinking alcohol or the use of illegal narcotics. This will further tend to impair their judgment and reasoning.

Again, there are several possible actions that may be taken when contact is made with poachers or when there is evidence of poaching. First, and again, be aware of your surroundings and your environment. Know what is going on around you.

If you do find signs that there is poaching going on, i.e. snares or other types of traps, leave the area immediately. Do not try to disarm the traps as you may be harmed. Preferably back track through the same route by which you arrived. By knowing the route that you came in and backtracking it, you will minimize the chance of activating any other traps that may be laid in the area.

If confronted by poachers, attempt to talk to them. Explain who you are and why you are there. Remember your purpose as a SAR crew member is not to act as law enforcement. You are there to locate and rescue the missing and endangered person(s). After you have reached a position of safety, immediately notify the Incident Command Post of the situation which you encountered.

SEARCHING ON PRIVATE PROPERTY

Search crews are called upon to search varied terrain in different sections of the country and world. We train to be proficient in all types of terrain. Incident Commanders and Search Crewleaders must take this knowledge one step further. They must know when and where search operations can be legally conducted. A lack of this knowledge could result in criminal charges and/or a civil action being brought against the search crews, Crewleaders and incident command staff.

Within the SAR community, it is understood that search is an emergency. However, this does not give SAR workers the absolute right to enter onto property or into buildings.

Legally speaking, the easiest areas to search are those owned or controlled by one entity. Examples would be national or state parks, large tracks of land owned or controlled by the same company or individual or any other location under singular control. To conduct a search in these areas, it is only necessary to obtain authorization to perform search operations from the one source.

When search operations will be conducted on several properties belonging to various owners, it is best to obtain authorization from a representative for each property. In open areas where there is no individual fencing or posting, this may not be possible because you cannot deter-

Chapter 4 - Crew Safety

mine where the boundaries are.

It is generally held that, if you are engaged in a search operation, acting in good faith, and cross from one unmarked or divided property to another, you would not be held criminally or civilly liable.

Obtaining authorization to cross into and search private properties should be obtained as quickly as possible at the onset of a search. Ideally this will be done by the Incident Command Staff. On government lands, normally the agency with control of the property will be actively involved. In the search operation, authorization is obtained from them.

Authorization to search an area can be either written or verbal. Usually it will be verbal. In either case, a log should be kept detailing the property in question, who gave authorization to search and the date and time permission was given.

When obtaining authorization to search, be specific as to the areas to be searched. If the area is all wooded or is open pasture, this is enough detail to note. However, if it is anticipated that there will be buildings on the property, mention them as well. If possible, have a means to contact a representative from the property to allow access to any buildings which appear secure. It is not unheard of for a victim to have either found a structure open or forced entry, then secured it from inside.

Most states in the United States allow forced entry into structures for emergency situations only. To satisfy this condition, the searcher would have had to have probable cause i.e. have reason to believe that it is more likely than not, that the victim is inside the structure and know that the victim is in immediate danger.

This can be a difficult test to meet. The preferred method to gain entry under emergency, as opposed to forced entry, is to either have the owner open the structure or give permission to force entry.

In all cases where forced entry is made, strive to cause as little physical damage as possible.

As a Crewleaders in the field, you may be confronted by a property owner. They may order you off of their property. Actions to take:

1. Attempt to explain that you did not know it was their property or how to contact them.

2. Make an effort to explain your purpose for being on the property.

3. Endeavor to obtain permission to continue the search.

Attempt to allay any concerns that may arise, i.e. damaging their fences, crops, etc. If they still order you off of the property, leave. Do not argue or fight with them. Contact Incident Command and have them work on obtaining authorization to search this property.

Law enforcement officers are an excellent resource for assistance in gaining access to various areas. In many jurisdictions, they will have lawful authority to enter private property. Many times citizens may be more cooperative granting permission to search if contacted by a law enforcement officer.

Each state has its own statutes which govern lawful access onto private property. As an Incident Commander or Crewleader, you must take the time to familiarize yourself with the laws in your area. Doing so will protect your crews and you.

DRUG PRODUCTION AREAS

Of the various man made hazards that may be encountered, illegal narcotics or alcohol production sites are the most dangerous. These can be found in just about anywhere throughout the United States. Incident Commanders and SAR Crewleaders must be aware of the potential dangers posed by these areas, and some basic precautions must be taken.

The operators of illegal narcotic or alcohol production areas are operating outside of established laws. Their basic motivation is greed. The narcotic producers will have large sums of money invested and huge profits at stake. Even the alcohol producers will normally have a fair sized investment with their livelihood at stake.

Most people have heard of marijuana being cultivated in rural areas and moonshine stills being set up. It is a misnomer to believe that these activities are small in scale. Neither are they limited to being found in rural areas.

SAR crews are becoming more involved in search operations in urban environments. The objects of these searches are typically missing children, endangered adults or persons lost in the aftermath of disasters, i.e., hurricanes, earthquakes, and floods. During these operations, SAR crews have the potential for being exposed to hazards previously encountered only by law enforcement and some fire personnel.

CRIMINAL MINDSET

Due to the criminal mindset and the amount of money involved, the operators of these areas will not hesitate to resort to violence to protect their investment.

The operators of narcotic or alcohol production areas will use various means to "protect their investment". These range from simple concealment and camouflage to armed guards and booby traps.

Rural Areas

Rural areas are most commonly associated with the illegal production of alcohol. The specific size of the area being used can vary from several hundred square feet to hundreds of acres. Production areas will normally be concealed within wooded areas or mixed in with other crops.

The approaches and perimeters of these areas will often be booby trapped in various ways. These booby traps are most commonly trip wires and pit traps. The trip wires may activate anything from a signaling device to an explosive charge or firearm. Pit traps are, as their name implies...pits dug in the ground. Usually narcotic producers will dig them just large and deep enough to step into. The intent may be to cause a twisted or broken ankle, or sharpened stakes may be placed in the bottom pointing up, to impale the foot.

Another less frequently encountered type of booby trap is similar in function to a military antipersonnel mine. These are planted in the ground at a shallow depth. When stepped on, they will detonate, maiming or killing. The devices themselves are normally small and may or may not have any parts visible.

Armed guards are also used to protect production areas. It must be remembered that they are engaged in a criminal activity. Their reaction to your presence will be unpredictable, and probably violent.

Urban Areas

Not as commonly encountered are production spaces in urban environments. In many large cities, illicit drugs are grown or manufactured indoors. This can be in a large warehouse, in a private residence, or apartment.

As in rural areas, threats of physical violence can be expected in urban areas. There are, however, heightened dangers associated with the urban production of narcotics.

The chemicals used in the production processes are often dangerous. When mixed together, they become very volatile. Many of these laboratories are slip shod and dangerous, at best. Chemicals are not properly stored and are improperly mixed. By and large, there are too many dangerous procedures to begin to list here.

There are a number of actions which can and should be taken by Incident Commanders and Crewleaders to protect themselves and their people.

1. Be aware of the potential for this type of activity in your search areas. Check with the law enforcement agency which has jurisdiction in that area. (Do not ask a road officer or deputy who may or may not know. They should be one source of inquiry, but not the only one.)

2. If there is a likelihood of this type of activity being in your search area, carefully weigh the risk/benefit factor. It may be better to have law enforcement officers search those areas.

Chapter 4 - Crew Safety

3. Fully brief your people.

4. Search Crewleaders and crews should pay constant attention to their surroundings.

5. If you accidentally stumble across a production area:
   a. Stop, go no further.
   b. Touch nothing. You do not know what may have been booby trapped. (i.e., Light switches have been wired to cause an explosion when turned on.)
   c. Immediately leave the area by the same route you arrived.
   d. Notify the Incident Commander.

Remember: You are a SAR worker but in the eyes of the operators of these facilities, you will be seen as a government representative and a threat. Avoid them.

ANIMALS

Wild animals may present hazards for the search crew during certain times of the year and in certain environments. Obviously, the best plan is to avoid contact, if at all possible. Most animals will avoid contact with the searcher, during most times of the year. Exceptions will be during breeding and/or birthing seasons for the animal. Males will generally become more aggressive during breeding season in an effort to establish and protect their territories. Females (particularly mothers) will aggressively protect the young.

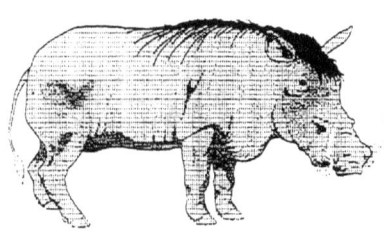

With some species, all females of that species will help guard the young in a "communal nursery". The best plan will be to know the breeding and birthing patterns for the wildlife that inhabits your area.

1. For the most part, making sufficient noise when moving through an area will alert any wildlife to your presence and they will attempt to move out of your way.

2. Avoid coming between a mother and her young.

3. Staying in groups will usually be safer than being alone when you have to be in the field during breeding and birthing seasons. Many animals will not challenge a "herd", but will show aggression toward individuals.

Working with a Search Canine may present special hazards when it comes to encounters with wild animals. Most competent Handlers will have trained with their Canines to assure that they will not "chase game" that may be in the search area. Further, the competent Handler should be assured that the Canine can be "recalled" reliably, before becoming operational with the Canine. However, Canines are animals and, on occasion, will revert to their instinctive drives when encountering wildlife in the field. More over, the wild animal may view the Search Canine as either a threat, or food, and may be attracted to the Canine.

Any time a Search Canine contacts a wild animal, the Canine should be quarantined until it can be determined that it hasn't contracted a disease from the wild animal!

1. Keep the Canine away from other Canines in base camp, and have it evaluated by a Veterinarian as soon as possible.

2. Do not rely on the fact that the Canine has been vaccinated. There are many strains of Rabies and, in some cases, one vaccine will be ineffective for the strain the Canine may have been exposed to from the wild animal.

Chapter 4 - Crew Safety   49

REVIEW QUESTIONS

1. List the five steps that a Crew Leader should take to assure that the crew does not become a part of the incident.
   _____   _____
   _____   _____
   _____

2. List the three steps that a Crew Leader should take to prepare the crew for weather emergencies.
   _____   _____
   _____

3. Define a Micro-burst. _____
   _____

4. List the steps that should be taken by the Search Crew when caught in a lightening storm in the outdoors.
   _____   _____
   _____   _____
   _____

5. List the three "Cold Weather Emergencies".
   _____   _____
   _____

6. List the four clothing layers used for thermo-regulation in cold environments.
   _____   _____
   _____   _____

7. List three steps that can be taken to avoid "Cold Weather Emergencies".
   _____   _____
   _____

8. List four steps that could be taken to rewarm individuals that are affected by the cold.
   _____   _____
   _____   _____

9. List the three "Heat Emergencies".
   _____   _____
   _____

Chapter 4 - Crew Safety

10. List three steps that could be taken to avoid "Heat Emergencies".

   _____   _____
   _____

11. How much water should the Crew Leader assure is available for the Search Crew?

   _____

12. Define the following for Forest Fires:

Fire Storm - _____

Crowning Out - _____

13. What three steps might be taken when encountering a Forest Fire in the wilderness?

   _____

14. List the three steps that should be taken when preparing for a search during hunting season.

   _____   _____
   _____

15. List the steps that should be taken by the Search Crew when they believe that poaching might be occurring in their search area.

   _____   _____
   _____   _____

16. When might a SAR crew have the lawful right to enter a structure without obtaining the owners permission?

   _____

17. List the steps that should be taken when confronted by an angry property owner who demands that you leave the property.

   _____   _____

18. List the steps that should be taken when there is suspicion of drug production activity.

   _____   _____

19. List the steps that should be taken when locating a drug production area during a search.

   _____   _____
   _____   _____

20. What should the SAR Crew Leader know ahead of time to avoid aggressive behavior from the wildlife that might be encounter in the field?

   _____

Chapter 4 - Crew Safety

21. List three steps that should be taken to avoid contact with wild animals.

    _____   _____

    _____

22. List the steps that should be taken when a Search Canine contacts a wild animal.

    _____   _____

NOTES:

SAR READY PACK FOR SAR TECH™ I AND SAR CREWLEADER III

OBJECTIVES

A. The student will be able to explain the difference between a 24-hour ready pack for SAR TECH™ I / SAR Crewleader III and a crew members 24-hour ready pack

B. The student will be able to list the SAR TECH™ I/SAR CREWLEADER III MINIMUM PERSONAL EQUIPMENT (See Attachment)

C. The student will have a 24-hour ready pack for SAR TECH™ I/ SAR Crewleader III and explain the use of its contents.

SAR READY PACK

The 24 hour or SAR ready pack is perhaps the most universal as well as individual topic covered in this text. A SAR pack becomes the searchers best friend or worst enemy on a search. A pack that fits poorly and is ill equipped becomes a burden - as does the searcher who carries it. A pack that is comfortable and well built, carries the items that allow a searcher to be efficient throughout a difficult search mission.

Search packs are usually dynamic in that each individual will attempt to try systems and equipment that make that "perfect" pack. Many searchers literally spend years of trial and error before settling down to a pack that they can live with and search with comfortably.

The minimum personal equipment list required for the SAR Ready Pack has been used through NASAR's FUNSAR courses and SAR TECH ™ certification. As the crewleader needs expanded knowledge and skills, so too is there a need for an expanded list for a crewleader pack. Amounts of some of the required items have been increased and other items have been added to the list. These items have been compiled from a sampling of search team requirements throughout the country and it contains the mandatory items common to almost all of those lists. Recent published articles in several "outdoor" magazines have focused on survival equipment for camping, backpacking and expeditions. All of these lists also include some or all of these items.

When looking at equipment carried by SAR responders, there are many items shared in common regardless of geographic location. A good example of this is the First Aid Kit required in the SAR ready or 24 hour pack. These kits are used for the searcher should an injury or medical problem occur involving the Crewleader or crew member.

During a search, even the most mundane event may affect the outcome of a search and the condition of a victim. A searcher with blisters affecting the feet will be less likely to concentrate on the task at hand. Because a medical problem becomes a major concern for the Incident Managers as well as the Crewleader, routine, as well as emergency first aid, must be dealt with quickly and efficiently.

The first aid kit is the most crucial element of these equipment requirements. For the Crewleader, this kit must be able to provide items needed for personal use as well as for the crew member emergencies. In a perfect world, all crew members would provide for their personal needs and should be checked for this equipment prior to each mission. As this does not always happen, a Crewleader must assume responsibility not only for his or her own personal safety, but also for the safety of crew members. For this reason additional amounts and some new items have been added to the list.

There are several items added to the list for the first aid kit that are additional to the original 24 hour pack lists.

First is the requirement for **antihistamine tablets**. Since the SAR Tech II standard was published, the availability of these drugs, over the counter, has become universal and allow them to be carried for the relief of symptoms related to allergic reactions. Caution must be used with this medication. Administer only the recommended dosage from the manufacturer and never administer to anyone allergic or suspected to be allergic to this medication. Be sure to check your _local medical protocols_ and follow them. A best scenario is to offer the drug to a crew member only when the member discovers

Chapter 5 - SAR Ready Pack

that they do not have a supply with them.

Also new on the SAR TECH™ I/Crewleader III list is the requirement for **surgical gloves**. These reflect the universal precautions prescribed by emergency services recognition that gloves are needed to avoid contact with body fluids which may carry infectious diseases. Gloves are a standard requirement for all fire, rescue and law enforcement providers who administer medical care or may contact body fluids. Many SAR Teams require this item as mandatory on equipment lists. It is recommended that these be the most durable type glove available to the individual, due to the harsh nature of the SAR environment. Two pairs are required and these are lightweight and inexpensive. If the lighter more fragile type are carried, it may be a good idea to add several more pairs in the kit. It is important to periodically examine these gloves if they remain unused in the pack for a length of time to ensure that they remain serviceable.

FIRST AID KIT

10	**Acetaminophen or aspirin tablets**	The number of these is increased to reflect the crew requirements.
10	**Antacid tablets**	The number of these is increased to reflect the crew requirements
10	**Antihistamine, 25mg Benadryl**	This item was optional in SAR Tech II.
6	**Antiseptic cleansing pads**	The number of these is increased to reflect the crew requirements
1	Antiseptic ointment (Tube)	No change from SAR Tech II
6	Band-Aids, various sizes	No change from SAR Tech II
1	Moleskin	No change from SAR Tech II
2	**Pair of latex gloves**	*New Item, see text*
4	**Roller Bandage**	The number of these is increased to reflect the crew requirements
1	Splinter forceps, tweezers	No change from SAR Tech II
1	**Scissors, multi-purpose**	This item was optional in SAR Tech II.
1	**Space blanket**	*New Item, see text*
4	**Sterile dressings (4x4 gauze pads)**	This item was optional in SAR Tech II *and* the number has been increased to reflect crew requirements
10	**Water purification tabs in sealed container or commercially approved purification device**	This item was optional in SAR Tech II *and* the number has been increased to reflect crew requirements

PERSONAL/CREW SURVIVAL KIT

1	Candle, long burning	No change from SAR Tech II
4	**Cotton swabs, non sterile**	The number of these is increased to reflect the crew requirements.
1	Duct tape, 5-10 ft.	No change from SAR Tech II
2	**Leaf bag, large**	The number of these is increased to reflect the crew requirements.
16	Matches	No change from SAR Tech II
1	Matches container, waterproof	No change from SAR Tech II
1	Plastic bag, zip lock, qt. size, for kit	No change from SAR Tech II
2	Quarters, for phone call	No change from SAR Tech II
1	Razor blade, single edge	No change from SAR Tech II
4	**Safety pins, large**	The number of these is increased to reflect the crew requirements
2	Towelette, clean	No change from SAR Tech II
1	Whistle	No change from SAR Tech II

PERSONAL/CREW SAR EQUIPMENT (continued)

4	Bags, various sizes, ziplocked	No change from SAR Tech II
1	Bandanna, handkerchief	No change from SAR Tech II
1	Cap or other headgear	No change from SAR Tech II
1	Clothes bag, waterproof	No change from SAR Tech II
1	Clothing, adequate for climate and environment	No change from SAR Tech II
1	Clothing, extra set, suitable for climate	No change from SAR Tech II
1	Compass, orienteering (Silva Ranger) or equivalent	No change from SAR Tech II
2	**Extra leaf bags**	Same as above but in a separate location
2	**Flagging tape, roll**	The number of these is increased to reflect the crew requirements.
1	Flashlight or lantern	No change from SAR Tech II
1	Flashlight extra, extra batteries and bulb	No change from SAR Tech II
1	Footwear, sturdy, adequate for climate	No change from SAR Tech II
1	**Gloves - Leather Palm**	Now mandatory
1	**Grid reader (UTM)**	*New Item, see text*
2	**ICS 214 Forms**	*New Item, see text*
1	Insect repellent	No change from SAR Tech II
1	Knife, multi purpose	No change from SAR Tech II
1	Lip balm, with sunscreen	No change from SAR Tech II
1	Measuring device, 18 in. minimum	No change from SAR Tech II
1	Metal cup or pot	No change from SAR Tech II
1	Mirror, small	No change from SAR Tech II
1	Nylon twine or small rope, 50 feet	No change from SAR Tech II
1	**Pace counter**	*New Item, see text*
1	Pack, adequate to carry required equipment	No change from SAR Tech II
1	Pad and pencil	No change from SAR Tech II
2	**Prussik cords (6MM-8MM) 6 ft. length**	*New Item, see text*
1	Rainwear, durable	No change from SAR Tech II
1	SAR personal identification	No change from SAR Tech II
1	**Safety Rope 75 ft. (one rescuer life line @ NFPA)**	*New Item, see text*
1	Shelter Material, 8x10	No change from SAR Tech II
1	**Sterno or stove**	This item was optional in SAR Tech II
1	Socks, extra pair	No change from SAR Tech II
1	Sunscreen lotion	No change from SAR Tech II
1	Tissue paper	No change from SAR Tech II
1	Tracking stick, 42" long	No change from SAR Tech II
1	Watch	No change from SAR Tech II
2	Water container, at least 1 liter size	No change from SAR Tech II
1	Webbing, 20 ft. length of 1 in. tubular	No change from SAR Tech II
1	Wire, 5-10 ft., 14 ga steel	No change from SAR Tech II

OPTIONAL PERSONAL SUPPORT EQUIPMENT. NOT REQUIRED, BUT RECOMMENDED

1	Altimeter	1	Gaiters	1	Sun glasses, 97% UV protection
1	Binoculars	1	Goggles, clear	1	Trail snacks
1	Foam pad	1	Protractor		
2	Food, non perishable	1	Rain cover, pack		

Chapter 5 - SAR Ready Pack

The requirement for **scissors** was based on the need to bandage and repair items in the field. Many responders had added this as a standard item in the pack even though it has been listed as optional. The medical type scissors found in most ambulance "jump boxes" work very well, however any multipurpose scissors will work fine.

Also, now required is the **space blanket**. After reviewing several SAR equipment lists it was noted that all of them required this item in the first aid kit. Additionally many SAR responders who were not required to carry this item did so anyway. There is sound reasoning for this requirement. Any person who becomes injured or ill in a wilderness environment needs to conserve body warmth and maintain a normal body temperature. A space blanket will help enable this to be accomplished during an emergency. The blanket can also serve the same function for a searcher who has become wet and risks hypothermia, or needs to reflect heat away from a patient in a hot environment by creating a reflective area of shade. The space blanket can also be used as an attraction device due to the shiny surface on one or both sides. This item remains fairly inexpensive and lightweight. Space type blankets come in a variety of configurations including the normal sheet style, a two sided "sleeping bag" type, as well as heavier weights with grommets used for suspending the blanket as a tarp or emergency shelter. This item has many properties that make it a sound investment and addition to the required items in a 24 hour pack.

Sterile gauze pads were also brought to the required list because of universal use by many agencies and teams. This item is indispensable for bleeding wounds and similar injuries.

Water purification tablets or chemical treatments have been identified as a need for SAR responders and are required by the SAR Tech™ II standards, however, there are many new filtering devices that have become reasonable alternatives for search responders, both in terms of cost, size, and function. These devices have been added to the list and should be investigated as a viable alternative to chemical treatments by any searcher who routinely must purify water in the field and who works in an environment where water is available in the field. Although the cost of these devices have become lower in the last few years, they may still represent a larger expense than most of the other items on the equipment list. They also may be quite large, depending on the type of design and construction. These devices may also require extended time to obtain usable amounts of water. Investigation and research are mandatory before the purchase of this item. Nearly all of the camping and equipment retailers offer a wide variety of filtering and chemical/filtering combination devices with new designs and features each month. Shop around for the item that suits your needs, which may be a bottle of iodine tablets.

In addition to the first aid kit requirements, SAR TECH™ I also requires several items related to the use of the new techniques being taught in the hazardous terrain section of the standard. Two carabiners, two Prusik cords, and seventy five feet of rope are now required for the crewleader to carry. These items are intended to allow the Crewleader to negotiate hazardous, non technical terrain by securing one end of a rope to a searcher and the other to an anchor point. The line is carried to the other side of the hazard and secured. This allows the other members to use a simple harness to secure to a safety line during a traverse.

The rope required to be carried should meet NFPA 1983 Standard for Life Safety Rope **One Rescuer Life Line** requirements. This means that the rope should be static kernmantle, with a working strength of 300 lb. and a breaking strength of 4500 lb.

The **Prusik cord** should be compatible to the diameter of rope carried, and be tied in a loop three feet in diameter from a cord six feet long. The knot should be a double fisherman's type or a figure eight follow-through. This Prusik is used to attach between the rope and carabiner

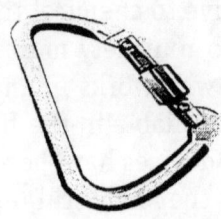

to secure the searcher.

The **carabiners** should be a locking gate type of a rated strength matching the rope requirements. No designation is made as to the type of metal or size of carabiner, as long as it is a locking type and large enough to allow a Munter hitch to function properly.

Gloves with a leather palm are intended to allow the Crewleader to belay and handle rope without injuring the hands. Many searchers carry a lightweight pair of leather gloves in the pack to protect the hands from rocks, briars, and other hazards to the hand.

Included on the list is a **UTM grid reader**. This handy device is a piece of plastic about two inches square and one sixteenth inch thick, that is scribed into a grid that fits UTM squares on a 1 to 24,000 scale topo map. By subdividing the UTM square with this grid and assigning numerical representations to a point, locations can be determined in the field. This square is available in several Search Equipment catalogues and from the bookstore at NASAR. See the land navigation chapter for instructions on its use.

A **pace counter** has been found to be invaluable in determining distances using the technique of pace counting or tally stepping. Many searchers use a set of "ranger beads or tally beads" for this function. However many also have found that a mechanical counter is easier for some people to use to keep track of the tally steps taken. This device is actually an inventory counter, a plastic or metal cylinder that counts by pushing a button. This can be used in pacing a distance by clicking the button each time the right foot hits the ground. Most searchers attach a lanyard to the counter and carry it on the wrist. Caution should be used with a metal counter when using a compass to assure that it does not deviate the compass magnet. These items are inexpensive and available at most office supply stores. Most searchers wonder how they ever paced without one once they have tried it.

The last new item is a member of the dreaded group known as "paperwork". Each Crewleader should carry two copies of the **ICS 214, Unit Log**, in the pack. Many times on a search there will be missions assigned in haste and this document is overlooked during a briefing. Indeed all documentation may be overlooked. Because the Crewleader assumes the responsibility for the crew, it is necessary to record and document the events of the crew during a mission. The unit log allows the Crewleader to record the incident name, date and time, crew designation, Crewleader, operational period, crew members name and home location, and a record of major events during a mission. This document is invaluable during a debriefing and allows the Crewleader to pass on accurate and valuable information that may otherwise not be recalled. A suitable way to carry and protect this paperwork must also be provided.

SUMMARY

Overall, experience shows that the concept of equipment requirements remain crucial to the success of a search. It is the responsibility of the searcher to carry the equipment needed to be efficient, effective, and self sufficient during a search mission. The Crewleader must assure that an example is set to other crew members and other searchers by always carrying a fully equipped pack on every mission. The Crewleader should also check the equipment carried by crew members.

Beneficial to the Crewleader is preparation for the additional weight and size of the SAR TECH™ I pack. The Crewleader should gain conditioning by carrying the pack in typical search terrain and becoming familiar with the contents and additional weight before it is required on a search or a SAR TECH™ I Exam.

Many searches would never have been successfully and safely completed if it were not for the preparation of equipment before the search ever began. Carrying and using a SAR ready pack will benefit **both** the searcher and the lost subject.

Chapter 5 - SAR Ready Pack

Below is a checklist, which may be photocopied for use in assembling and maintaining the pack.

Personal/Crew First Aid Kit

- ☐ 10 -Acetaminophen or aspirin tablets
- ☐ 10 -Antacid tablets
- ☐ 10 -Antihistamine, 25mg Benadryl
- ☐ 6 -Antiseptic cleansing pads
- ☐ 1 -Antiseptic ointment (Tube)
- ☐ 6 -Band aids, various sizes
- ☐ 1 -Moleskin
- ☐ 2 -Pair of latex gloves
- ☐ 4 -Roller Bandage
- ☐ 1 -Splinter forceps, tweezers
- ☐ 1 -Scissors, multi-purpose
- ☐ 1 -Space blanket
- ☐ 4 -Sterile dressings (4x4 gauze pads)
- ☐ 10 -Water purification

Personal/Crew Survival Kit

- ☐ 1 -Candle, long burning
- ☐ 4 -Cotton swabs, non sterile
- ☐ 1 -Duct tape, 5-10 ft.
- ☐ 4 -Leaf bag, large
- ☐ 16 -Matches
- ☐ 1 -Matches container, waterproof
- ☐ 1 -Plastic bag, zip lock, qt. size, for kit
- ☐ 2 -Quarters, for phone call
- ☐ 1 -Razor blade, single edge
- ☐ 4 -Safety pins, large
- ☐ 2 -Towelette, clean
- ☐ 1 -Whistle

Personal/Crew SAR Equipment

- ☐ 4 -Bags, various sizes, zip locked
- ☐ 1 -Bandanna, handkerchief
- ☐ 1 -Cap or other headgear
- ☐ 2 -Carabiner, locking gate
- ☐ 1 -Clothes bag, waterproof
- ☐ 1 -Clothing, adequate for climate and environment
- ☐ 1 -Clothing, extra set, suitable for climate
- ☐ 1 -Compass, orienteering (Silva Ranger or equivalent)
- ☐ 1 -Dividers - (compass type)
- ☐ 2 -Extra leaf bags
- ☐ 2 -Flagging tape, roll
- ☐ 1 -Flashlight or lantern
- ☐ 1 -Flashlight extra, extra batteries and bulb
- ☐ 1 -Footwear, sturdy, adequate for climate
- ☐ 1 -Grid reader (UTM)
- ☐ 2 -ICS 214 Forms
- ☐ 1 -Insect repellent
- ☐ 1 -Knife, multi-purpose
- ☐ 1 -Lip balm, with sunscreen
- ☐ 1 -Measuring device, 18 in. minimum
- ☐ 1 -Metal cup or pot
- ☐ 1 -Mirror, small
- ☐ 1 -Nylon twine or small rope, 50 feet
- ☐ 1 -Pace counter
- ☐ 1 -Pack, adequate to carry required equipment
- ☐ 1 -Pad and pencil
- ☐ 1 -Protractor
- ☐ 2 -Prussik cords (6MM minimum - 6 ft. length)
- ☐ 1 -Rainwear, durable
- ☐ 1 -SAR personal identification
- ☐ 1 -Safety Rope 75 ft. (one rescuer life line @ NFPA)
- ☐ 1 -Shelter Material, 8x10
- ☐ 1 -Sterno or stove
- ☐ 1 -Socks, extra pair
- ☐ 1 -Sunscreen lotion
- ☐ 1 -Tissue paper
- ☐ 1 -Tracking stick, 42" long
- ☐ 1 -Watch
- ☐ 2 -Water container, at least liter size
- ☐ 1 -Webbing, 20 ft. length of 1 in. tubular
- ☐ 1 -Wire, 5-10 ft., 14 ga. steel

Optional Personal Support Equipment recommended

- ☐ 1 -Altimeter
- ☐ 1 -Binoculars
- ☐ 1 -Foam pad
- ☐ 2 -Food, nonperishable
- ☐ 1 -Gaiters
- ☐ 1 -Gloves, even in summer
- ☐ 1 -Goggles, clear
- ☐ 1 -Rain cover, pack
- ☐ 1 -Sun glasses, 97% UV protection

REVIEW QUESTIONS

1. The ICS form #_____ is a new requirement for the SAR TECH™ I/Crewleader III ready pack.

2. What is this ICS form used for? _____

3. The SAR TECH™ I ready pack should contain enough equipment for the _____ and _____ .

4. The best way to prepare for carrying the SAR TECH™ I pack is to:
   _____

5. One reason for additional equipment requirements for the SAR TECH™ I/Crewleader III is to assure the _____ of the crew.

6. List the two new items required on the first aid kit list for SAR TECH™ I.
   _____   _____

7. List four of the new items required on the Personal/Crew SAR Equipment list for SAR TECH I.
   _____   _____
   _____   _____

NOTES:

MAPS, SYMBOLOGY AND LAND NAVIGATION

OBJECTIVES

A. The student shall be able to list the common maps used by land SAR personnel, aircraft search crews, and other SAR resources.

B. The student shall identify the different common coordinate systems and describe the common elements between them.

   1. Latitude and Longitude

   2. Universal Transverse Mercator grid system

C. The student shall identify the photo revised sections of a USGS topo map.

D. The student shall describe the use of a back azimuth in locating a position.

E. The student shall demonstrate the ability to locate a position on a map, using a resectioning method.

F. The student shall demonstrate the use of tools and techniques used to determine road, trail, and straight line distances on a map.

G. The student shall demonstrate the ability to navigate accurately around an obstacle blocking the path of travel.

H. The student shall demonstrate the ability to navigate an extended course at night, wearing his/her SAR TECH™ I ready pack, using a compass, map, grid coordinates, and terrain features for a distance of not less than fifteen hundred (1500) meters and not more than two thousand (2000) meters.

I. The student shall demonstrate a technique used to adjust a compass bearing for degrees of declination.

J. The student shall define and demonstrate the use of ICS symbols and markings used with land search maps.

MAPS, SYMBOLOGY AND LAND NAVIGATION

Land navigation is an indispensable skill for the SAR worker, especially a crewleader. It is ultimately the crewleader's responsibility to accurately lead his/her crew during a crew assignment. Being in the wrong place during a search assignment can totally defeat the effectiveness of search planning, as well as be embarrassing if discovered. Imagine a SAR crew finding a clue or an injured subject and not being able to relay their location to the Command Post! As with most skills, navigation competency will only be achieved through constant practice. It is up to each individual to perfect his/her navigation skills by continuously training with the tools and materials he or she will be using on actual SAR assignments.

Because SAR personnel are often called to search areas they are unfamiliar with, map reading and compass navigation skills are absolutely essential. Such situations also create a need for standardized navigation resources and methods in the SAR community.

In this chapter, the material is oriented towards land based search and rescue crewleaders. It is assumed that you have had some exposure to basic map reading, compass use and navigation. Although some material may be remedial, emphasis is placed on skills and knowledge a crewleader should have.

This chapter is not a comprehensive guide to navigation. The material presented covers information NASAR feels is optimum for land search and rescue. With this material, we hope to standardize navigation techniques and resources used between SAR agencies, thus allowing more efficient cooperative search efforts.

MAPS FOR SEARCH AND RESCUE

A map is basically a two dimensional, graphic representation of a section of the earth's surface. It provides representations of: directional orientation, distance, physical features, and relative position. Currently, there are many types of maps available for various purposes. For a map to be useful, it must contain information pertinent to the needs of the user.

Proper map selection for SAR is vitally important. For instance, if we are trying to navigate on land in an urban area, an aeronautical chart would be of little value, since it would not show street names. This is obviously a poor choice of application — a city road map would be a better choice. Preplanning should prevent a situation like this from happening. A search team should have maps of their jurisdiction suitable for the type search they will conduct. In the real world we are sometimes forced to use whatever is available.

The following is a review of maps commonly available to, and used by SAR personnel.

Planimetric maps, such as road maps, show both natural and man-made features such as roads, waterways, and buildings. These maps, though widely available, vary in scale from one area to another and show very little about terrain features. This makes these maps undesirable for wilderness field use. They may, however, be useful for some aspects of a SAR incident, such as logistics or by units assigned to confinement of a search area.

Site specific maps for areas such as state parks, wildlife management areas, national forests, hiking trails or other recreational areas are maps that are available for SAR use. These maps are produced in a variety of formats by groups ranging from hiking clubs to government agencies. As a result, they vary in scale and feature detail. While some of these maps may be good enough to be useful to SAR workers, they are hardly universal.

Fire Service maps, which are sometimes used by local Emergency Services, often find their way into SAR use. These maps give more terrain detail than most planimetric maps, but are charted to a scale smaller than is desirable for foot travel. They can be useful when coordinating operations between multiple agencies who may already be familiar with these maps.

Aerial photographs provide an excellent representation of most geographical features, but have a number of shortcomings for SAR workers. First, scale is sometimes hard to determine or

Chapter 6 - Maps, Symbology & Navigation

not even known. Second, if the photograph was taken while summer foliage was present, subtle features may be obscured and terrain may not be well represented.

Surveyors' maps are generally available for most any areas, but should be used only when no other maps are available. These maps show virtually no terrain features and a very limited amount of roads or trails. The scale on these maps also varies widely.

Aeronautical charts are available for most anywhere and are scaled consistently. However, they contain only a limited amount of information useful for ground travel, especially on foot. The scale used on these maps is also too small to be practical for the foot traveler. These maps would have only a limited benefit to a land search operation.

Topographical (topo) maps are the most frequently used maps for land-based search and rescue. These maps are readily available for most any area. The United States Geological Survey (USGS) produces these maps in a number of scales, two of which, the 7.5 minute and 15 minute maps, work well for SAR use. These maps contain detailed representations of natural and most man-made features. The 7.5 minute quadrangle map, scaled 1:24,000, is well suited for the foot traveler and is the optimum map for land search and rescue. Because of its usefulness, the topographic map will be discussed in greater detail later in this chapter.

Orthophoto quads are a cross between aerial photographs and topographic maps. They are photographed to an exact scale consistent with standard topographic maps and are labeled as topo maps would be, with the exception of contour (elevation) lines. Peak elevations such as hill tops are typically noted. These maps are quite useful for search and rescue, however they are not available for all areas.

MAP READING

As we have already pointed out, topographic maps are the primary maps of choice for land based search and rescue because of their excellent terrain and feature detail, good availability, and standardized format. This being the case, SAR crewleaders need to be proficient at reading and understanding topo maps.

To begin to understand maps, we first need to know about coordinate systems representing the area of the earth being mapped. The two coordinate systems we are concerned with are: Geographic Coordinate System (Latitude/Longitude), sometimes referred to as "true coordinates", and the Universal Transverse Mercator (UTM) grid system.

LATITUDE / LONGITUDE

The Geographic Coordinate System is commonly known as Latitude/Longitude. Longitude is represented by a system of imaginary lines running from the north pole to the south pole of the earth. **(See Figure 6.1)** Latitude is represented by a system of imaginary rings encircling the earth perpendicular to the north-south lines. **(See Figure 6.1)** Latitude can be defined as an angular distance, in degrees, relative to the equator. Latitude provides the north/south component of a geographic position. Longitude is defined as an angular distance, in degrees, relative to the prime meridian. Longitude provides the east/west component of a geographic position.

The equator represents 0° (zero degrees)

Figure 6.1

Latitude and the Prime Meridian which runs through Greenwich, England represents 0° Longitude. These are the starting points for lat/long positioning. Latitude can range from 0°, at the equator, to 90°N, at the north pole, or 90°S, at the south pole. Longitude represents divisions of a circle (the equator), so its range is theoretically 0° to 360°. In actuality we use the longitude line directly opposite of the prime meridian as a limit for east or west location. This longitude line is referred to as the International Dateline. Since the prime meridian is 0°, the international dateline is 180°. Therefore, longitude can range from 0°, at the prime meridian, to 180°E or 180°W, at the international dateline.

Coordinates are expressed numerically as angles and divisions of angles. Example: 35° 44' 30" (35 degrees, 44 minutes, 30 seconds). You may remember from geometry that angles are divided into minutes and seconds — e.g., 1° = 60 minutes, 1 minute = 60 seconds. In some cases, coordinates are expressed in degrees and decimal minutes instead of degrees, minutes, and seconds. Example: 35° 44.50' (35 degrees, 44.50 minutes).

The protocol for expressing a coordinate in latitude/longitude is to indicate the position north or south of the equator (Lat) first, then indicate the position east or west of the prime meridian (Long). A typical expression of lat/long coordinates for a location in North Carolina would read: 35° 44' 30" N, 79° 39' 07" W.

Several things about lat/long are important for SAR personnel to know. One important consideration is the fact that Longitude (used to determine East/West position) lines grow closer together as they near the poles of the earth. This creates problems in defining linear distance relative to angular measure. For instance, 1° of longitude at 0° latitude (the equator) is equal to roughly 69 miles straight line distance. At 36° N latitude, which runs through the lower half of the continental United States, 1° of longitude is equal to approximately 56 miles. At 85° N latitude, which is close to the north pole, 1° of longitude is only equal to about 6 miles. Due to this deviation, we do not have a simple plotting device for determining longitude on maps.

Another factor affecting SAR use of lat/long coordinates is the accuracy of plotting points on a map. This is due in some part to the situation described in the previous paragraph. In addition, a great deal of skill and a correctly scaled device is needed to accurately plot points using lat/long. If a point is plotted to 1" (1 second) of accuracy on a 7.5 minute topographical map, the point is accurate to within approximately 31 square meters, at best. This is certainly close enough for SAR use, but plotting to 1" of accuracy on 7.5 minute maps is unrealistic. Plotting a point to 15" (15 seconds) of accuracy is much more realistic and even this can be tough to accomplish, especially in the field. A point plotted to 15" accuracy will locate a point within approximately 460 square meters, which is not as close as we would like.

While it is obvious that the lat/long coordinate system is not ideal for SAR use, we do need to be familiar with it. This system is globally universal and can be used between most all types of organizations world wide. Aircraft and marine vessels use this system for navigation, especially in conjunction with electronic guidance systems such as Loran and GPS (Global Positioning System). There may be a time when SAR personnel will need to give a location to an aircraft crew in lat/long coordinates. As hand held GPS receivers become more popular with SAR agencies, this will become easier to do. Much more could be said about latitude/longitude positioning, however this is not the primary navigation system of SAR workers, so we will move on.

UNIVERSAL TRANSVERSE MERCATOR (UTM)

Now that we have a fundamental understanding of the Geographic Coordinate System, we can discuss the Universal Transverse Mercator (UTM) grid system. The UTM system is a metric system of coordinate measurement. The nomenclature of the metric system seems to intimidate many of us non-Europeans. However, in map usage this is not a problem. The only units of measure we are concerned with are: meters and kilometers. Their relationship is very easily explained: 1 kilometer = 1000 meters. Since the metric system uses multiples of 10 (base 10) as its foundation, it is easily expanded or divided to fit our needs. With UTM, this can be used to produce the most practical scale for the map application we want.

An important characteristic of the UTM grid system is, unlike latitude/longitude, UTM north/south lines do not converge. They remain parallel over the entire map. This produces consistently scaled grid squares at all points on the map. Geographic points can be plotted from these grids with a device similar to a ruler, which we will discuss later in this chapter.

The UTM system does not use angular measurements to report geographic position as with the latitude/longitude system. Instead, linear measurements in meters are used. The equator is the origin for the northerly coordinate component in the northern hemisphere and the termination for the northerly coordinate component in the southern hemisphere. This is to allow navigators in both hemispheres to determine northerly position by working from south to north. The International Dateline (180° Long) is used for the origin of easterly position reporting. Notice we said easterly, not east/west.

The UTM system divides the circle created by the equator into 60 segments or zones. Each zone is equal to 6° longitude (360° ÷ 60 = 6°). The zones are numbered 1 through 60 starting at the International Dateline and moving from west to east. **(See Figure 6.2)** Therefore, the International Dateline is the westerly border of zone 1 and the easterly border of zone 60.

The reason for using such narrow segments is to minimize the curving distortion of the north/south lines (as discussed earlier) when the area is flattened and projected in two dimensions. Since the north/south curved distortion becomes the greatest near the poles, there is a limit to how close to the poles the UTM system will work. Because of this, the zones extend to only 84° N latitude in the northern hemisphere and 80° S latitude in the southern hemisphere.

If we take a 6° UTM zone, flatten it and view it in two dimensions, we notice the longitude lines that form the east and west boundaries of the zone are curved slightly. **(See Figure 6.3)** The longitude line in the middle of the zone, the central meridian, is straight and perpendicular to the equator. The equator and central meridian of each UTM zone are used as the basis of the UTM grid for each respective zone.

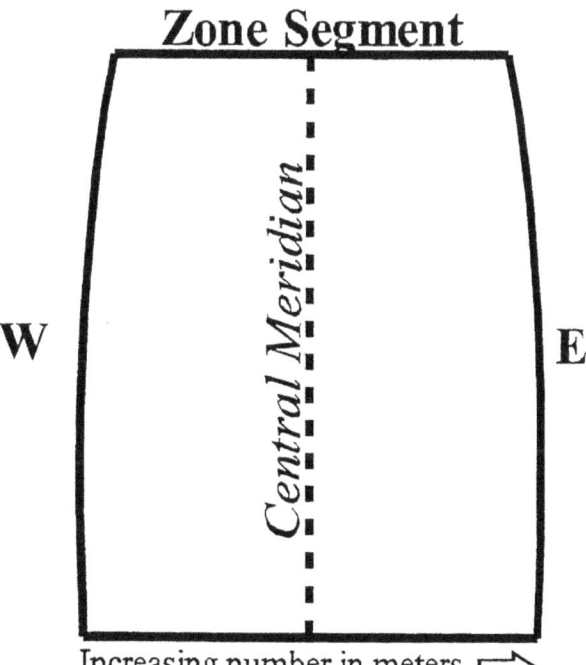

Figure 6.3

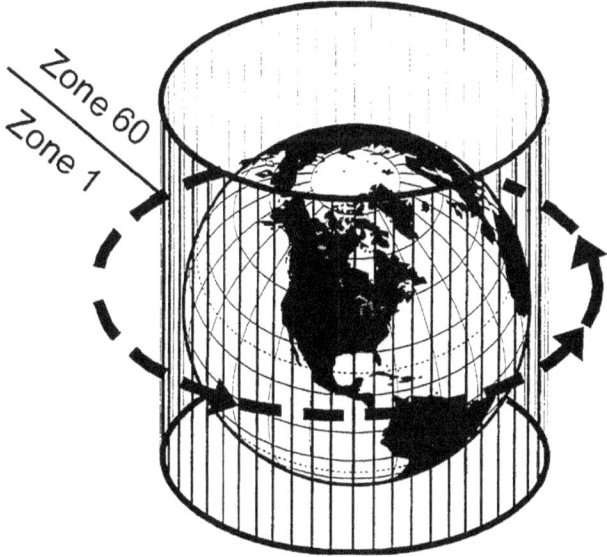

Figure 6.2

Incidentally, the central meridian of each UTM zone is also used as the basis for the easterly coordinate numbering for that zone. The central meridian for each zone is arbitrarily given the number 500000 mE (500,000 meters). UTM grid lines west of the zone's central meridian will have decreasing numbers. The numbers decrease until they reach the border of the next UTM zone (the numbers do not necessarily reach zero). Grid lines east of the zone's central meridian will have increasing numbers until they reach the border of the next zone. This creates a numbering system that increases from the west side of a UTM zone all the way to the east side of the zone. Consequently, easterly UTM coordinates are always read from west to east.

The protocol for expressing UTM coordinates is to indicate the easterly position first and the northerly position second. More about this will be discussed later in this chapter.

Cartographers must make allowances to correct for the distortion that occurs within a UTM zone. When zones are divided to produce maps of smaller areas, such as the 15 minute or 7.5 minute topo maps, the projection contains very little distortion. The corrections on these maps can cause a deviation from true north. That is why true north and grid north references are given on a map. This will be explained in greater detail later in the chapter.

The United States Geological Survey incorporates the UTM grid system into their topographical maps. The 7.5 minute topo maps have 1 kilometer grids, which are easily subdivided using simple measuring devices. By subdividing these map grids, we can consistently plot a position on a map to within ± 20 meters (65 feet) or closer with ease, even in the field. This obviously makes the 7.5 minute topo map and the UTM grid system ideal for SAR use.

To summarize what we have learned about coordinate systems, we know that latitude/longitude and the UTM grid system have several common features, including:

- The equator is the basis for determining north/south position with both systems.
- Both systems contain a variation between their respective north reference and magnetic north.
- Both systems use the International Dateline (180° long) as a reference.
- Both systems allow us to determine our relative geographic position.
- Both systems allow us to determine a direction of travel.

We have also learned that there are several distinct differences between the lat/long system and the UTM grid system, including:

- The lat/long system uses angular degrees to describe geographic position while UTM uses linear distance.
- The protocol for describing a latitude/longitude position is to describe the north component of a position first then the east or west component, whereas in UTM we give the easterly position first then the northerly position.
- Latitude position can be reported as north or south (depending on which side of the equator we are on). UTM only reports a north position.
- Longitude position can be Reported as east or west (depending on which side of the Prime Meridian we are on), while UTM only has easterly positions.
- The lat/long system covers the entire earth, while the UTM system extends to only 84° N latitude (in the northern hemisphere) and 80° S latitude (in the southern hemisphere).UTM north lines remain parallel on maps but lat/long lines grow closer together as they get closer to the poles of the earth (depending on map area size and scale)

TOPOGRAPHIC MAPS

We have determined that topographic maps, with the type and amount of information they contain, and the UTM grid coordinate system provide the optimum map resource for land search and rescue. At this point, we need to discuss in more detail the information found on topo maps.

Map Scale

Throughout this chapter, we have referred to 15 minute and 7.5 minute topographic maps. These numbers basically refer to the size of the geographic area represented on the map.

A 15 minute map will display an area that is 15 minutes latitude by 15 minutes longitude, or 1/4 degree square. In linear distance this is roughly 17.25 x 17.25 miles at equator (the distance west to east will decrease farther from the equator). Because of the large amount of area shown on this map, the scale (1:62,500) is smaller than is practical for the foot traveler. These maps may be useful for a large scale SAR incident or by aircraft crews who may be covering a large amount of area.

A 7.5 minute map will display an area that is 7.5 minutes latitude by 7.5 minutes, or 1/8 degree square. In linear distance this is roughly 8.6 x 8.6 miles(the distance west to east will decrease farther from the equator). Since the area covered by this map is not excessive, the scale (1:24,000) is large enough to provide reasonably well detailed features. Short distances that a foot traveler might cover can be easily measured and plotted at this scale.

INFORMATION FOUND ON A TOPO MAP

The actual size of 7.5 minute maps is 27 inches high by 21 inches (will vary according to north latitude) wide. These maps can be folded down to a size that is easy to manage in the field without compromising the map features. 7.5 minute maps are readily available for most areas from the United States Geological Survey, outdoor outfitters, and local map shops at a cost ranging from $ 4.00 to $ 8.00. The 7.5 minute topographic map is the optimum map for land SAR and the one we will concentrate on throughout the remainder of this chapter.

MAP FEATURES

Features found on topographic maps fall into four categories; Terrain, vegetation, hydrography, and culture. The use of color plays an important part in representing these features. Without color, topo maps can be difficult to interpret. For this reason, black and white photocopied topo maps should be avoided if possible.

This chapter describes only a limited amount of symbology. **(See Figure 6.8)** The United States Geological Survey prints a color guide for topographic map symbols. This guide is available at no charge from USGS and many retail map outlets. A map symbology guide is a highly recommended item for crewleaders to carry.

Terrain

Terrain, or topography, is represented on topo maps through the use of **contour lines**. These are brown lines that represent elevation

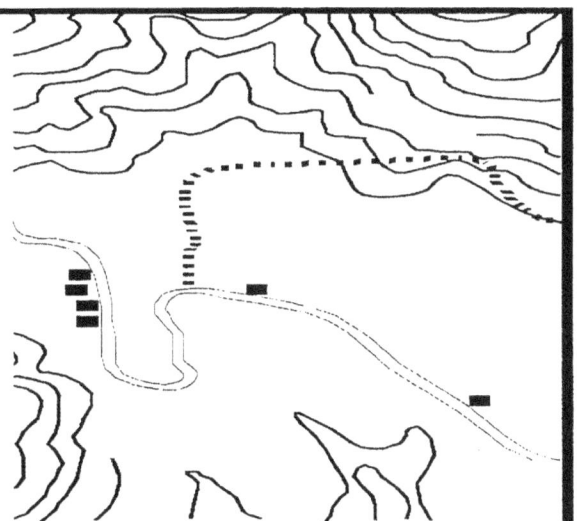

Figure 6.4

above sea level. The lines are drawn to follow the shape of the actual geography by connecting geographic points having the same altitude. **(See Figure 6.4)**

Contour lines will run somewhat parallel to other contour lines, with every fifth line being a darker shade of brown. The darker contour line, known as a **contour index**, will have a number indicating its altitude. The value of the distance between the parallel contour lines is referred to as the **contour interval.** This value can be found in the center of the bottom margin of the map, usually below the map distance legend. The amount of space between the contour lines indicates the severity of the terrain. Con-

Figure 6.5

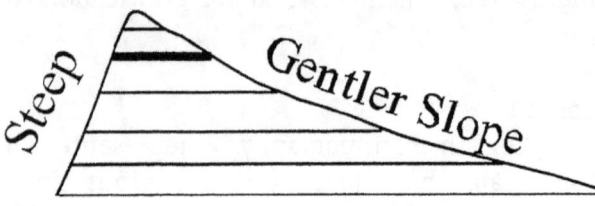

Figure 6.6

tour lines very close together indicate steep terrain, while contour lines that are far apart indicate gently sloping terrain. **(See Figure 6.5 & 6.6)**

The shapes the contour lines are drawn to also indicate terrain features. For instance, pro-

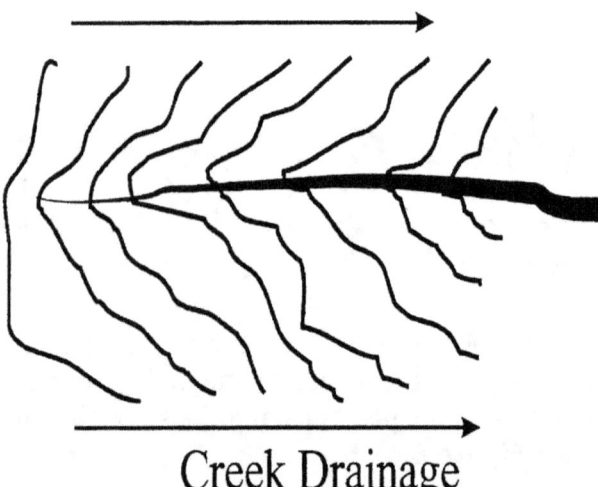

Figure 6.7

gressively closer parallel contour lines indicate a hill or mountain. Contour lines drawn to produce a "U" or "V" shape indicate a drainage or valley. **(See Figure 6.7)**

Reading contours from a map is often a difficult concept to grasp. Complete proficiency will only come through diligent practice in the field. This skill must be mastered by anyone wishing to be a SAR crewleader. Reading contour from a map is a crucial component of map/ terrain orientation.

Bjorn Kjellstrom, in his book Be Expert With Map and Compass, suggests an exercise to help understand the concept of contour lines. In this exercise, a rock is used as a miniature geographic feature. The base of the rock is dipped 1 inch into a pan of water and removed. A line is then drawn around the rock at the top of the water mark. The base of the rock is then dipped 2 inches down into the water and removed. Another line is drawn around the second water mark. This process is repeated until the entire rock has been contoured. One can now see contour lines in three dimensions. By looking straight down at the top of the rock, one can also see what a two dimensional map view would be. This exercise can be quite useful in grasping the concept of map contour.

VEGETATION

Vegetation is represented on topo maps with a combination of symbols and color. Wooded areas are shaded in light green. Non-wooded areas such as fields are not shaded and will be white. Areas having scrub growth are shaded with randomly placed light green dots. Certain agricultural areas such as vineyards and orchards are represented by rows of symmetrically placed green dots. Wooded swamp or marsh areas have green shading plus symbology showing vegetation. **See Figure 6.8** for more symbology relating to vegetation on topo maps.

HYDROGRAPHY

Hydrography (water) is shown on topo maps in a light blue color. Bodies of water can range from a wet weather drainage to a large lake or ocean. There are many symbols used on topo maps that are associated with water. For a complete listing of these symbols, **see Figure 6.8** or the USGS guide to topographic map symbols.

CULTURE

The term "culture", as it applies to mapping, refers to anything in the map area that has been affected by civilization. Culture generally implies buildings, roads, trails, power transmission lines, cemeteries, bridges, etc. Culture

Chapter 6 - Maps, Symbology & Navigation

can also refer to such things as man-made alterations to the terrain, borders or boundaries, survey control monuments, etc. By far, the majority of all map symbology is dedicated to describing cultural features. **(See Figure 6.8)** This particular aspect of mapping is the one most subject to change. SAR personnel need to be acutely aware of possible changes that could affect the accuracy of their map.

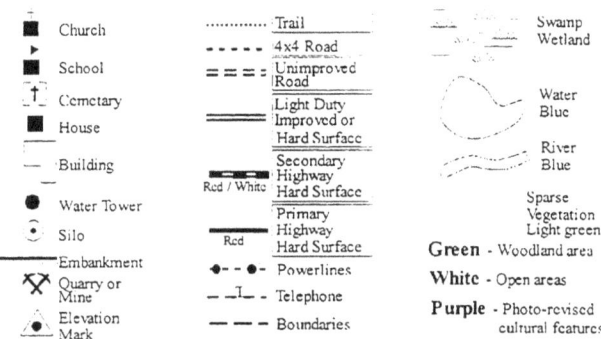

Figure 6.8

Because of cultural changes USGS will, from time to time, update maps. Often this is done through a process called photorevision. A photorevision is done by comparing a recent aerial photograph with an existing map. Changes are noted on the map in purple. A map that has been photorevised will have a photorevision date included in the map legend. This date is usually located in the lower left and/ or lower right corner of the bottom margin of the map.

Often maps are photoinspected, but no revisions are necessary. In this case, there will be no purple photorevisions shown on the map. Instead, a photoinspection date will be shown in red. This date is also found in the corners of the lower map margin.

Maps without recent photoinspection/ photorevision dates should be verified by SAR personnel as part of area preplanning. If a map with no recent photoinspection or photorevision must be used, all field personnel should be so advised in mission briefings.

MAP DIRECTION ORIENTATION

A topographical map usually contains three directional references. They are true north, grid north and magnetic north. These references can be found in the lower margin of the map in

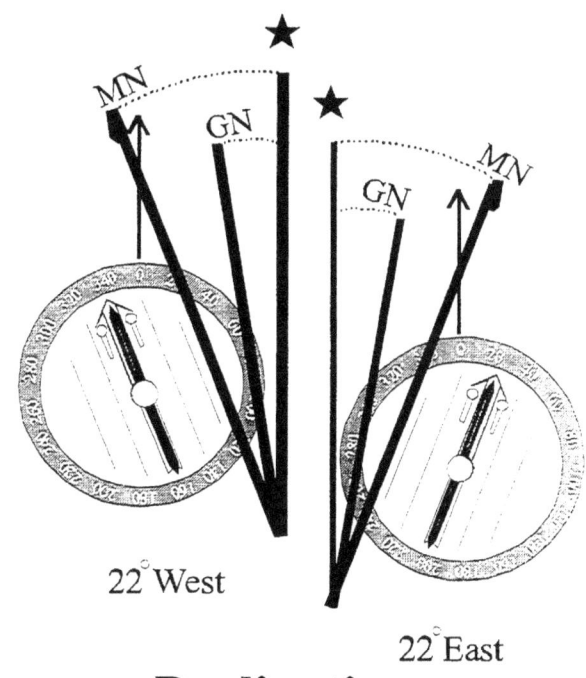

Declination

Figure 6.9

symbolic form. **(See Figure 6.9)**

As you can see from **Figure 6.9**, the north reference symbol uses abbreviations to indicate the north references. True north, Indicated by a star (★), is the direction to the geographic north pole of the earth (the northerly convergence of all longitude lines). This is typically the north reference used by most other maps.

Grid north, indicated by the letters "GN", is the north reference the UTM grid is aligned to on the map. Grid north usually varies only a couple of degrees or less from true north. In many cases the amount of variance is less than a whole degree. **(See Figure 6.9)**

Magnetic north is indicated by the letters "MN". Magnetic north, sometimes called "compass north", is the direction to the magnetic north pole of the earth. This is the direction the north needle of a magnetic compass will point. It is important to remember that the geographic north pole and the magnetic north pole of the earth are not the same.

Since there is variation between the three north references, we must be aware of exactly which north reference to use. When we work from the UTM grid on the map to determine direction of travel, we are using grid north. When we use our compass to navigate in the field, we are using magnetic north. Because there is a difference between the two, we must adjust for the difference when determining compass headings, performing map resections, etc. This variation between grid north and magnetic north is called magnetic declination. If we do not adjust for declination, compass headings determined from the map will be incorrect for field use and vice versa.

Magnetic declination, sometimes referred to as the grid-magnetic (G-M) angle, is best described as the total angular difference between grid north and magnetic north. This will be the amount of adjustment we need to make to our compasses or compass headings (covered later in this chapter). We seldom reference true north in SAR work. Declination can be easterly or westerly depending on where we happen to be. To determine the direction of declination from the map legend, we observe the relationship of grid north and magnetic north. Declination is said to be westerly if magnetic north is west of grid north. **(See Figure 6.9)** If the opposite is the case the declination is easterly.

Magnetic north changes slightly over time, therefore, magnetic declination changes as well. That is the reason a date is shown beneath the north reference legend on the map. **(See Figure 6.9)** Maps without recent revisions may be slightly inaccurate regarding declination, but the difference is usually inconsequential. Since we seldom have a way of knowing the amount of change, this date is generally ignored and the declination shown is used.

MISCELLANEOUS TOPO MAP INFORMATION

Topographical maps contain a great deal of information in the map margins. **Figure 6.10** shows the top margin of a topo map. The top right corner shows the name of the map quadrangle, as well as the state and county (or parish) location. The map series is also shown in the top right corner (e.g., 7.5 Minute Topographic). The information written diagonally at the corners of the map is the names and designations of adjoining quadrangles. The information in small red print shows the destination, as well as distance to the destination, of a road. The red print, usually accompanied by a red arrow, is typically adjacent to where a road contacts the map border.

Coordinates in degrees, minutes and, in some cases, seconds are shown at both top corners of the map. These are the latitude/longitude coordinates of each respective map corner.

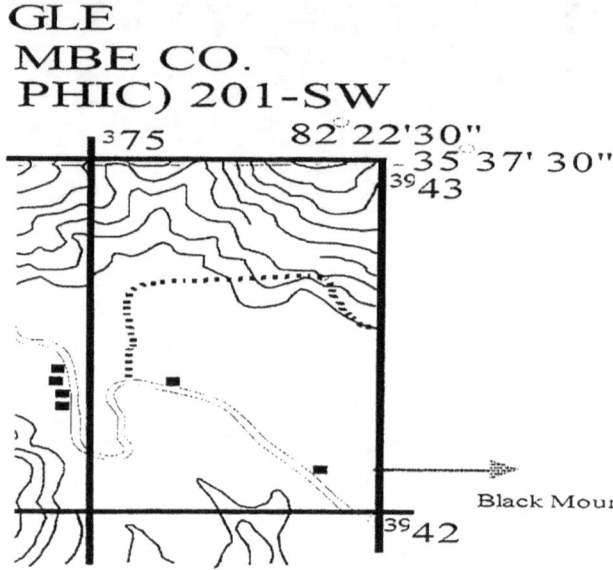

Figure 6.10

The number on top is the longitude and the number below is the latitude. Longitude is also shown in two other places across the top map border. **(See Figure 6.10)** Usually these longitude coordinates are shown only in minutes or minutes and seconds. Directly beneath these longitude coordinates will be a black tick mark extending from the map border into the map area about 1/8 inch.

Also across the top of the map will be groups of numbers spaced approximately 1 5/8 inches apart. These numbers begin with one or two numerals in smaller case and are followed by one or two numerals in larger case. Often the first of these numbers (far left) will have three smaller case zeros and the letters "mE" following the large case numerals. This number is the easterly UTM grid coordinate for the map and represents XXX,000 meters east. The other numbers not having the zeros and "mE" lettering are also easterly UTM grid coordinates, but have

Chapter 6 - Maps, Symbology & Navigation

been abbreviated. The numbers progress proceeding from left to right (west to east). A light blue tick mark can be found beneath each of these numbers. The tick extends from the border of the map into the margin (approximately 1/8 inch). The actual distance (over land) between each tick is one kilometer (1000 meters).

The bottom margin of a map **(See Figure 6.11)** provides the most information to the map user. In the lower right corner, the quadrangle location is shown, with corresponding latitude/longitude coordinates. Beneath the quad location, the map date followed by a photorevision or photoinspection date (if applicable) is shown. Directly above the quadrangle name, a legend showing road classification is often shown.

The map scale is shown in the center of the bottom margin, followed by a map distance legend. Directly beneath the distance legend is the map contour interval (described earlier). To

OTEEN, N.C.
35082-E4-TF-024

1962
PHOTOREVISED 1990
DMA 4555 III SW-SERIES V842

Bottom right of map

Figure 6.11

the left of the distance legend is the north reference. **(See Figure 6.9)**

Information including map date, map reference datum, and UTM zone can be found at the lower left corner of the map. If a map has been photoinspected or photorevised, the revision date will be at the bottom of this information block.

Latitude/longitude coordinates are shown across the bottom of the map much as they are in the top map margin. The difference between coordinates in the top margin and bottom margin is in the order they are shown. At the top corners of the map, the coordinates are given with the longitude above the latitude, at the bottom corners they are reversed with the latitude above the longitude. The longitude coordinates across the bottom and top of the map are identical.

UTM coordinates and grid ticks shown across the top margin are also repeated in the lower map margin. They too will have the identical numbers.

Information concerning names and designations of adjoining quadrangles can be found written diagonally near the lower map corners. In addition, the name of the quadrangle immediately south of the map is found in the center of the lower margin directly above the map scale. The name will be in parenthesis, written in black ink.

The side margins of a map contain information for UTM and lat/long coordinates represented in the same fashion as the top and bottom margins. **(See Figure 6.12)** The numbers along the sides give the north or south longitude position and the northerly UTM grid position. The UTM grid numbers are also abbreviated along the sides of the map, with the exception of the top number in the left margin and the bottom number in the right margin. Both UTM and lat/long coordinates will have the grid ticks described earlier.

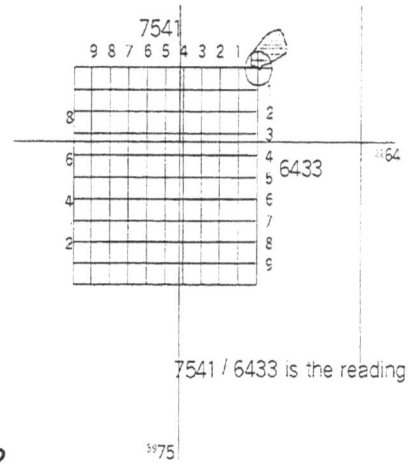

Figure 6.12

The side margins will also have the names of adjacent maps. They can be found half way between the upper and lower corners. Road destinations and distances are also shown in the side map margins.

PREPARING A TOPO MAP FOR SAR USE

Before a topographical map is ready to be used by search and rescue personnel in the field, several things must be done. Recently dated topo maps often have the UTM grid already on the map. Older maps seldom have the grid on them, therefore it is the responsibility of those in the planning section to do this. If, however, a crewleader is one of the first on scene, he or she may be the one having to do this.

Gridding a 7.5 minute topo map is quite simple. All that is needed to do this is a fine point, black, ball point pen and a 30 inch long straight edge (preferably metal — to avoid flexing). Align the straight edge with a blue UTM tick at the top of the map and the corresponding UTM tick at the bottom of the map. Be sure to allow for the width of the pen point when aligning the straight edge with the tick marks. This will ensure that accurate grid lines are drawn. Once the straight edge is aligned, simply draw a line connecting the ticks. Be careful not to make the lines too heavy or dark. Heavy lines can alter the accuracy of the grid as well as obscure subtle map features.

Repeat this process for all UTM ticks across the top and bottom of the map to complete the north/south grid lines. Use the same process to draw the east/west grid lines using the blue UTM ticks along the side of the map.

Another item that needs to be added to all SAR topo maps is the magnetic north lines. We will need a protractor (a large size protractor is best) and a 30 inch straight edge to do this. First, we must determine declination from the map (described earlier). Once we know the amount and direction of declination, mark a reference point on the east/west UTM grid line near the bottom of the map (a grid intersection can be used). Align the index mark at the center of the protractor base with the reference mark. Keeping these aligned, align the horizontal protractor index (0° line) to the east/west grid line. The 90° index on the protractor is now aligned to grid north. Starting from the 90° protractor index, make a mark on the map at the edge of the protractor corresponding to the degrees of declination. Be sure to move in the proper direction (east or west) away from the 90° index on the protractor. Do not use the lower map border instead of the UTM grid line for the east/west reference line. This will create an incorrect grid north reference.

Once magnetic north has been marked, the protractor can be removed from the map. Now, align the straight edge with the initial reference mark and the mark made at the edge of the protractor. Draw a line up the map from the bottom border all the way to the next border the straight edge intersects. To add more magnetic north reference lines, align one edge of the straight edge with the previously drawn north line. Using the other side of the straight edge, draw a line connecting the bottom map border to the map border intersected by the opposite end of the straight edge. Repeat this process until the map has enough magnetic north lines. Once again, be careful not to make these lines too heavy or dark.

As mentioned earlier, SAR preplanning should include field verification of maps, especially older maps. Cultural changes may need to be hand drawn on maps by SAR workers. This can be a good exercise for SAR teams to stay familiar with areas within their jurisdiction.

ORIENTEERING TOOLS

The tools a crewleader should have for field map reading include, as a minimum, an orienteering compass and a UTM grid reading device.

The orienteering compass can be used as a protractor for determining compass headings on a map. Numerous compass models are available from several companies. Most all are adequate for SAR work.

The UTM grid reading device needs to be scaled 1:24,000, for use with 7.5 minute topographical maps. The grid reader should divide the 1 kilometer grid square into ten smaller horizontal units, and ten smaller vertical units. If the grid reader subdivides these ten units further, that is even better (provided it can be read easily). There are several versions of UTM grid reading devices available. Ideally, the grid reader should be small enough and durable enough to be carried in the SAR ready pack. **Figure 6.12** shows one type of grid reader commonly used by SAR personnel.

PLOTTING COORDINATES ON A TOPO MAP

In FUNSAR, we learned a technique to plot UTM grid coordinates on a topo map. Through observation of field searchers, it seems that this skill may need to be reinforced. Here we will briefly review this skill using the grid reader. **(See Figure 6.9)**

If we have marked a point on the map and need to determine its UTM coordinates, the procedure is as follows:

Find the closest north/south grid line to the left (west) of the point. Follow the line to either the top or bottom of the map and note the UTM number for this line. Now, align the left side of the grid reader to the vertical UTM grid line. While maintaining the vertical alignment, align the bottom of the grid reader to the closest east/west UTM grid line beneath the point. Once the grid reader is completely aligned, locate the closest vertical grid reader line to the left of the point. Count the grid reader lines (starting at the first line to the right of the UTM grid line) over to this line. This line should be included in the count. Note the counted number with the number previously noted.

To obtain the final number, we must interpolate the distance between the grid reader line to the left and right of the point on the map. Imagine that the small grid reader square (in which the point lies) is subdivided with ten vertical lines. Estimate which of these imaginary vertical lines would intersect the point and note the respective number.

Now that we have all of the numbers needed, they must be organized. When we note the first number (from the top or bottom of the map), we typically omit the first (lower case) number(s) and use only the upper case numbers. For example, if the number shown on the map was 436, we would only note 36. We noted the next number from counting the grid reader lines. This number would be placed behind the numbers noted previously. For instance, if we counted seven lines, we would put the number "7" behind the "36" giving us the number 367. The interpolated number is handled in the same fashion. If we estimated the number within the grid reader square to be five, we would put the number "5" behind the "367" giving us the number 3675.

The easterly component of the UTM coordinate has now been established, but we must go back and determine the northerly component. This is accomplished with the same procedure used for the easterly component. The difference is now we will use the horizontal map and grid reader lines.

First, find the closest horizontal grid line beneath the point on the map. Follow the line to either side of the map and note the UTM number for this line. Now, align the bottom of the grid reader to the horizontal UTM grid line as we did before. While maintaining the horizontal alignment, align the left side of the grid reader to the vertical UTM grid line used earlier. Once the grid reader is completely aligned, locate the closest horizontal grid reader line beneath the point. Count the grid reader lines (starting at the first line above the UTM grid line) up to this line. This line should be included in the count. Note the counted number with the number previously noted.

To obtain the final number, we must interpolate the distance between the grid reader line above and below the point on the map. This is accomplished in the same fashion as the easterly coordinate, only vertically.

Remember, the protocol for reporting UTM coordinates is to give the easterly coordinate first, northerly coordinate second. For instance, if the northerly coordinate we just located was

"5326", the entire position would be reported as 3675 / 5326. In relation to the map, just remember left to right then bottom to top. Since this protocol is universal, we do not designate "east" or "north" when writing or verbalizing UTM coordinates. Occasionally, coordinates will be stated with east and north only having three digits each. A coordinate stated with three digits is accurate to within 100 meters. This is usually close enough, but by including the fourth digit we narrow the accuracy to within 10 meters. This is obviously more desirable for search and rescue purposes. With practice, this kind of plotting accuracy can be repeated consistently.

If we are given a set of coordinates and need to plot the corresponding point on a map, the procedure is virtually the same. The first thing to do is locate the UTM grid lines that match the first digits of both the easterly and northerly coordinates. Next, we align the grid reader to the respective UTM grid lines as we did earlier. From here, we perform the procedure previously described.

DETERMINING DIRECTION OF TRAVEL AND DISTANCES ON A MAP

As a SAR TECH™ I/Crewleader III it is your responsibility to ensure a proper direction of travel. This chore can be delegated to a competent individual on your team and is encouraged. That will leave you free to look after all functions of your assigned mission, but as crewleader, the ultimate orienteering responsibility will be yours.

To be a crew leader you should be proficient with a map and compass. You should be able to tackle any navigational problems that may occur during the course of the mission. When unable to successfully navigate an assigned search area, valuable time is lost, P.O.D. [Probability of Detection] and P.O.A. [Probability of Area] can not be accurately calculated, and the total search operation is hindered.

The whole point of the SAR TECH™ programs is to standardize the training and certification levels of all participating NASAR members. When a search and rescue effort is acted upon in any part of the world, the local search manager will know what type of resources he or she has available.

Sometimes you will be exposed to geographical areas other than your own. You should posses the level of skill to navigate comfortably and accurately in these circumstances.

NAVIGATION TECHNIQUES

As we all know when we are participating in a search that entails a large area it is conceivable that your crew may be dropped off somewhere besides the correct starting point. It is the crewleader's responsibility to make sure that this does not happen and is easily avoidable if you will do a few orienteering checks. If you have G.P.S. (Global Positioning System) capabilities it would be advisable to see if the current coordinates displayed on your G.P.S. match the coordinates of those of the drop off point. Another check that could be done would be orienting your map to the terrain with the use of your compass. This can be accomplished by rotating the bezel on the compass to a heading of 360 degrees. Then place the Westerly or Easterly edge of the compass base plate on the magnetic north lines (which should be drawn on your map). If they are not drawn on your map this directional line is available in the margin area at the bottom of your topo map. Now rotate your map, with compass affixed to map, until your magnetic north needle is lined up parallel with the orienting arrow beneath it. Now you should be able to observe the features in the surrounding terrain and apply them to the map.

When you are assigned to a mission in a search and rescue effort, you will be called upon to navigate in many different ways. If you are in a mountainous region or an area with many defined features (e.g., ridge lines, creeks, rivers, drainages, logging roads, etc.), you will probably be assigned to guide your crew through a search area following one or more of these features. The reason we follow these defined features is that they give us a good point of reference so as to know our present location. Lost

Chapter 6 - Maps, Symbology & Navigation

subject statistics seem to suggest that people who are lost will also follow these features. This increases the possibility of finding clues and ultimately finding the lost subject.

If you are assigned to lead a crew in a somewhat flat area or an area without many defined features, it will probably be necessary to shoot an azimuth or bearing. An azimuth is a direction that can be stated in compass degrees with magnetic north being the control. If you get to a point in your mission that requires you to go back to your previous position, this can be done by shooting a back-azimuth. A back-azimuth can be accomplished two ways. First, on your compass turn your bezel 180 degrees from your present direction of travel, now line up your magnetic north needle with your orienting arrow. You have just completed one way of shooting a back-azimuth. The other method of shooting a back azimuth would be to leave the bezel in its current position. Now rotate your body around, with compass in hand, until your magnetic north needle is lined up with the opposite end of your orienting arrow. Following either one of these procedures will allow you to accurately shoot a back-azimuth.

While you are navigating on a mission it may be necessary to get an accurate fix on your present location. It may be that you have located a clue or possibly the subject you were looking for and need to notify someone. An excellent technique for accomplishing this task is what is known as a **map resection**. To perform this technique you first need to orient your map to the terrain. Now look carefully at your surroundings. Try to find a minimum of two prominent features such as a mountain, road junction, or large structure that is identifiable on your map. Using your compass shoot a bearing at a feature that is visible to you at this time and document your azimuth. Now locate this feature on your map. Affix your compass on the map so that the orienting lines in the center of your compass are parallel to the magnetic north lines drawn on the map. Now align the edge of the compass so that it crosses over the center of the designated feature. Strike a line with a marker along the edge of the compass extending from the feature toward your location. Repeat this same procedure with the next feature you have chosen. You will now find an intersection that you have drawn between these points on your map. Take your available grid reading device and place it over the intersection to arrive at the coordinates you were trying to obtain using the map resection method. It is important to remember that compass declination has to be set on 0° when performing a map resection using magnetic north lines. If UTM grid lines are used as the north reference you must account for declination accordingly.

NAVIGATING AROUND OBSTACLES

Sometimes during a mission you may encounter an obstacle such as a body of water, an impassable thicket, or sheer cliff that will not allow you to continue on your present course. In such cases, without proper resources, you must navigate around these obstacles to preserve the safety of the crew.

If you can see across the obstacle (e.g., small body of water), shoot an azimuth to the other side of the obstacle and pick out a prominent landmark which lines up with that azimuth. Walk around the obstacle until you locate the landmark you targeted from the other side. Check your compass heading and continue on with your assigned mission. If keeping up with your straight line distance is crucial to your mission, this method may not be recommended.

If the obstacle you encounter is too large or too dense to see through, a different navigational approach for traversing the obstacle may be necessary. **(See Figure 6.13)** The "Right Angle Method" would be as follows: (1) take a heading which is 90 degrees from your current azimuth; (2) using your new heading, accurately tally off the number of paces it takes to clearly pass beyond the extension of the obstacle; (3) turn 90 degrees and travel parallel to the obstacle until you have passed beyond it; (4) turn 90 degrees back towards the original azimuth and count off the same number of paces you tallied in step number 2; (5) turn 90 degrees in the direction away from the obstacle and continue on your original azimuth. If your mission requires you to keep up with total distance traveled, add only the distance traveled in step number 3 to the distance traveled prior to reaching the obstacle.

If you are proficient with map and compass and have had GPS training, this is an excellent scenario to apply this technology to your search and rescue efforts. A GPS, given the cor-

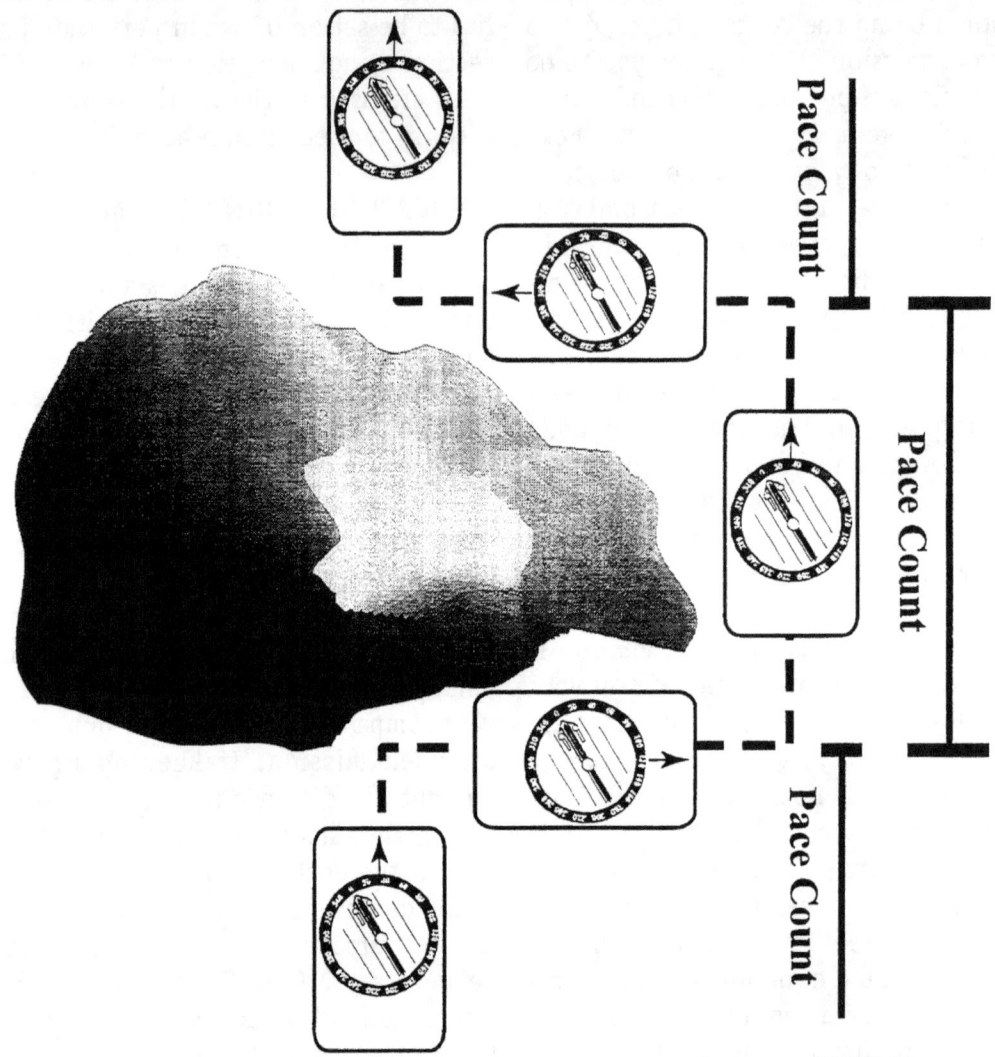

Figure 6.13

rect coordinate information, will steer you around an obstacle without having to worry about errors that can occur while doing the right angles method as mentioned above. Another advantage of GPS is all crew members are free to involve themselves in the clue finding process because GPS navigation can be done at a glance with proper training and some practical experience.

NIGHT NAVIGATION

During most organized search and rescue operations the onset of darkness does not stop the search effort. Actually in some situations it is easier to search at night. For instance, NASAR's lost subject statistics tell us that people who are lost have a tendency to either stop or slow down their pace drastically during the confines of darkness. Anyone who has taken a course in tracking realizes the benefits of working after sunset. Using artificial lighting, such as flashlights and lanterns, you are able to manipulate shadows therefore making footprints and disturbances more pronounced.

The problem with searching at night is that navigating during darkness is more difficult than during daylight hours. If your mission requires you to follow a defined feature, the task is usually not that difficult. However, if you get to a point where you are not quite sure of your location and need to perform a technique such as a map resection this could prove to be very troublesome.

Several considerations need to be taken when trying to maintain a bearing during a night mission. Since your line of sight is shorter at night, it stands to reason that you will have to pick closer reference objects when sighting your compass. This makes your rate of travel slower than it would be during the day. It may even be necessary to send a crew member ahead of the search party to shoot an azimuth towards when the terrain you are searching has no tangible reference points. Searching while maintaining a compass heading during the darkness is a challenge but can be accomplished if your compass is outfitted with luminescent features and you have experience at night navigation.

Another point to be addressed about night navigation is that while you are concentrating on your compass you have a natural tendency to drift downhill while walking across sloped terrain. If you are aware of this you can correct for it by taking a slightly upward trek to compensate.

ADJUSTING A COMPASS BEARING FOR DECLINATION

Adjusting for declination is a field technique that a SAR TECH™ I/ Crewleader III may have to implement during his/her search career. On most organized search missions the command staff would not allow you to begin a mission without a topo map of your search area that has the UTM grid and magnetic north lines on the map. On occasion, you may have to utilize this skill if you are summoned to participate in a search and rescue effort with an ill prepared search organization that does not have properly prepared maps. It may, in this case, be necessary for you to temporarily or permanently adjust your compass for declination depending on circumstances and type of compass you are using.

Should a map not have magnetic north lines drawn in and you are forced to adjust your compass for declination, remember one simple rule — EAST DECREASE - WEST PROGRESS. This will apply when we make a temporary adjustment to a compass heading. In other words, if declination is easterly we would subtract the declination from our compass bearing. If declination is westerly, we would add the declination to our compass bearing. For example, if you are in Thermopolis, Wyoming, the topo map shows magnetic north to be 14° east of grid north meaning that the magnetic declination is 14° easterly. Using the rule of declination above, you would know to subtract 14° from the azimuth determined on the map as you set your compass. In another example, Norfolk Virginia has a declination of 8° westerly. Using our rule of declination, we would know to add 8° to the compass azimuth.

Some brands of compasses will allow you to do what is known as a permanent declination adjustment on the compass. The point of this feature is to allow you to correct for declination on the bezel so as to not have to remember to add or subtract every time you shoot a bearing. See the instruction manual with your compass to correctly adjust for declination if it is equipped with this feature.

It is important to remember that setting declination in the field is only done as a last resort. Search teams who know the value of preplanning will have their topo maps with the UTM grid and magnetic north lines in place. As long as all searchers are working off of 0° declination, the chance for error is greatly decreased.

Chapter 6 - Maps, Symbology & Navigation

REVIEW QUESTIONS

1. List the maps that are commonly used for Search and Rescue.
   _____   _____
   _____   _____
   _____   _____
   _____

2. Topographical Maps are printed in _____ scale and _____ scale.

3. Two coordinate systems that are useful with Topographical Maps are:
   _____
   _____

4. Coordinate positions that are reported as angular measure describes the:
   _____

5. Coordinate positions that are reported as a measure of linear distance describes the:
   _____

6. Positions for the geographic coordinate system are reported _____ first, then _____ second.

7. Positions for the UTM coordinate system are reported _____ first, the _____ second.

8. Brown lines printed on the USGS Topographic map indicate _____.

9. Photorevisions to the USGS Topographic map are indicated by the color _____.

10. Green areas on the USGS Topographic map indicate _____.

11. Hydrography is indicated on the USGS Topographic map by the color _____.

12. The elevation difference between adjacent contour lines describes the _____.

13. Magnetic declination is the difference between _____ and _____.

14. Direction expressed in degrees with magnetic north as the control describes an _____.

Chapter 6 - Maps, Symbology & Navigation

15. Describe the method for applying a bearing from the map (using GN as the control) to the compass, in an area with 120 degree westerly magnetic declination.

_____

_____

16. List two ways for determining a back azimuth:

_____

_____

17. Describe the method for locating a position using resectioning.

_____

_____

18. Describe "the right angle method" for navigating around obstacles encountered in the field.

_____

_____

NOTES:

SEARCH TECHNIQUES AND TACTICS
OBJECTIVES

A. The student shall be able to define Probability of Detection (POD).

B. The student shall be able to describe the factors that have an effect on the crew's Probability of Detection (POD).

C. The student shall be able to describe scanning and observation skills and techniques.

   1. Clue awareness
   2. Relevant and irrelevant clues
   3. Scanning vs Observing
   4. Scanning ranges
   5. Increasing observation effectiveness

D. The student shall define critical spacing and explain how it is used.

E. The student shall identify the different types of searches, describe their differences, and demonstrate the techniques for maximizing the effectiveness of the following:

   1. Hasty searches (route or segment)

      a. Objectives of hasty searches
      b. Types of resources used for hasty searches
      c. Hasty search formations
      d. Crew duties and assignments

   2. Efficient searches

      a. Objectives of efficient searches
      b. Types of resources used for efficient searches
      c. Formations for efficient searches
      d. Spacing for efficient searches
      e. Crew duties and assignments

   3. Thorough Searches

      a. Objectives of thorough searches
      b. Types of resources used for thorough searches
      c. Formations for thorough searches
      d. Spacing for thorough searchese.
      e. Crew duties and assignments

4. Signcutting Tactics
   a. Objectives of signcutting tactics
   b. Types of resources used for signcutting tactics
   c. Signcutting PLS or LKP
   d. Signcutting routes
   e. Signcutting perpendicular to a suspected direction
   f. Signcutting around clues

5. Confinement and attraction tactics

F. Dog/Crew Searches

1. The student shall define the different types of search dogs and describe the uses of each type.

   a. Air scenting dog
   b. Tracking dog
   c. Trailing dog
   d Avalanche dog
   e. Cadaver dog
   e. Disaster dog
   c. Water search dog

2. The student shall define the differences between scent discrimination and non-scent discrimination trained dogs and list the advantages and disadvantages of each.

3. The student shall describe the role of the search crew in supporting a dog crew and the role of the dog crew in supporting the search crew.

4. The student shall describe the effects of the following on Tracking/Trailing and Airscenting dogs.

   a. Wind
   b. Weather
   c. Terrain
   d. Time of day

5. The student shall describe the search strategy considerations when using SAR dogs in the following types of searching:

   a. Hasty searches
   b. Efficient searches
   c. Thorough searches

SEARCH TECHNIQUES AND TACTICS

SEARCH THEORY AND STRATEGIES

This is a brief review of search theory and modern search strategy. Search theory changed when it was determined that the emphasis of a search should focus on the many clues that were generated by a search subject rather than on the subject. Along with this change in focus, the Point Last Seen (PLS) and Last Known Point (LKP) took on a major importance in determining search strategies.

Search theory is based on the Probability of Area when multiplied by the Probability of Detection will equal the Probability of Success.

PROBABILITY OF AREA

(POA) is the probability that the subject will be in a particular area. All of the segments of the potential search area, along with the "Rest Of World" (ROW), are assigned a number greater than zero percent but less than 100 percent. All assigned POAs must total to exactly 100. The POA is used as a planning tool which the search manager uses to determine where to assign limited search resources.

PROBABILITY OF DETECTION

(POD) is the probability that clues will be discovered in an assigned search segment by a specific search resource. How well a search resource can or has searched a segment is expressed by the POD. POD can be also thought of as a way to determine the search effort or "concentration" in a particular segment or the total area. The POD is a probability number ranging for 0 to 100 percent. The POD may be used as an assigning tool which a search manager uses to specify the search effectiveness of a search resource.

PROBABILITY OF SUCCESS

(POS) is the probability that the search subject will be found in a certain segment utilizing a certain level of searching concentration. The POS is another planning tool which the search manager utilizes to help in the determination of resource allocation. The POS is the product of POA multiplied by the POD. That is, POS = POA X POD.

SEARCH STRATEGIES

Search Area Minimization Strategy - mandates that any search area must be restricted in size and, if at all possible, be prevented from growing. Once that strategy is understood, the search area or potential search area can be further minimized by using other various strategies.

Search Area Confinement Strategy - One of the immediate goals of search is to reduce or eliminate the possibility of the lost subject leaving the established search area. Establishing confinement around the perimeter of the search area by utilizing passive and active tactics should be accomplished as shortly as possible after the first notice.

Establishing the Direction-of-Travel Strategy - An investigation and search of the PLS (Point Last Seen) may determine the direction of travel of the lost subject. PLS is a good starting point to launch a search as it is certain that the subject was at that location. However, the PLS is not the only place where determining direction of travel may be found. The discovery of clues throughout the search area may also yield the traveling direction of a lost subject.

Binary Search Strategy - The theory behind the binary search strategy is to divide the search area into smaller segments that can be searched effectively by search resources. Then search the perimeters of the segments with highly trained search resources. Even if the resources searching the perimeter do not find any clues you may be able to lower the POA (Probability of Area) in some adjoining segments because of the lack of clues found that would indicate movement of the lost subject between segments. This strategy would continue until the clues of the subject are found and the POAs indicate a more specific segment to search.

Prioritizing Search Segments Strategy is a management tool used to prioritize segments by

POA importance. This gives the Incident Commander a tool to help determine which segments need to be searched first and which segments can be searched last. This prioritizing is a "fluid", and time-dependent process. It will change as information about the search updates. Clues found or not found will affect this prioritizing.

Further information on search theory and strategies are covered in the NASAR *Managing the Lost Person Incident* (MLPI) course and NASAR *Planning Section Chief* course.

PROBABILITY OF DETECTION (POD) - IT IS THE CREWLEADER'S RESPONSIBILITY TO ACCURATELY DEVELOP THE POD FOR THE SEARCH RESOURCE HE OR SHE IS LEADING.

PROBABILITY OF DETECTION (POD)

Many things will affect the calculation of Probability of Detection: effects of the environment, the tactics being utilized by the resource (search crew), and the search techniques of the individuals assigned to the resource

The environment will greatly affect the POD of any search resource. The amount of light (natural or man-made) will have a definite effect on how effective a search resource will be. The amount of available light of course, is directly related to how much the searcher can see, and therefore anything that reduces searcher vision reduces the effectiveness of that searcher. Many times, a daylight search is far easier than a nighttime search. Cloud cover, snowy, rainy, or foggy weather, vegetation and ground features will obscure vision and hamper clue finding.

Search crews affect their POD in many cases by the tactics they use. Some tactics are used to rapidly search large segments while others are used to concentrate the search effort in very small areas of a segment. The larger the search segment, and the faster the search resource is asked to search the segment, the lower the POD. The teamwork of the crew in accomplishing the search tactic can also have an effect on the POD.

Searcher Techniques can effect the POD of the search crew. The individual skill levels of the crew members has an accumulating effect on POD. One of these skills is the techniques used by searchers to find clues. Each searcher could think of him/herself as one link in a chain of search efforts to find the lost person.

SEARCH TECHNIQUES

Search techniques are the search skills used by an individual to look for clues and to find the lost subject. In addition, techniques are used by all of the members of a search crew to carry out the planned tactics of searching a segment. No matter how good the tactics and strategies are in theory, they will only work when each searcher applies good search techniques.

When we examine the specific search techniques of an individual searcher we must recognize that there are two distinct aspects of searching techniques. The first is the physical technique involved in looking for clues and subjects. We call the physical aspect, **"scanning"**. The second, and equally important but often overlooked technique is the mental factor. We call the mental aspect, **"observing"**.

CLUE AWARENESS

The first step in clue awareness is your personal preparation. You must be in the right mind-set to search. This means that during the pre-planning component of SAR, you will have to tend to your health and physical conditioning. In addition, your nutrition and hydration status before and during the search assignments will also greatly effect your clue awareness. A very important preparatory factor in clue awareness is your experience and training. Training for clue seeking in an environment similar to your response environment will certainly increase your personal probability of detection.

The second step in clue awareness is mission preparation. Besides the obvious preparation of gear and equipment, you must acquire as much information about the mission as possible. Knowing who your search subject is and what his/her possible clues and habits may be, will "tune" your observational frequency to a most likely "channel" to discover clues.

Chapter 7 - Search Techniques and Tactics 87

The third step in clue awareness is to prepare for observing. You must prepare your mind by concentrating on the job at hand. You must keep your mind open to what the search environment will soon be telling you. That is to say, once you depart for your search assignment, you must set yourself in the "search mode". The reason for this is that there have been actual cases where an overexuberant search crew zoomed past critical clues on their way to their assigned search area! Always be aware that you may pass important clues in transit to and from an assigned search area. Always be alert for clues until you have returned to your Incident Base.

Your clue awareness should be tuned to all four possible categories of clues. Those clues may be 1) physical, 2) recorded, 3) people, or 4) events. Keep your mind open and do not fall victim to preconceived notions which could prejudice you about the facts of what has happened, what the clues may be, or where the lost subject may be.

One additional comment on clue awareness concerns your personal morale during the search assignment. If you have been searching for several hours through nasty weather, your ability to observe clues will be dramatically diminished. When you and your crew become fatigued, balancing your sense of humor with your professionalism will go a long way towards maximizing the effectiveness of your crew.

CLUE RELEVANCY

Typically, a search area will contain the clues left by passing human beings, animals, and in some instances, vehicles. Our objective is to sift through all of those clues to find only the clues which are meaningful or relevant to our specific search. One of the greatest challenges for a searcher is to discriminate between the clues left by the subject, and the clues left by the passage of unrelated animals, vehicles, or humans. Judging between what is important and what is meaningless is called "clue relevancy".

The primary source of relevant clues is the pre-search briefing. The briefing should provide you with both a written and a verbal source of possible clues. The written source comes from a document known as a Lost Person Questionnaire. Keep in mind that the Lost Person Questionnaire will never be "complete," but it will certainly provide you with some information about your subject(s). In addition, knowing the lost person profile will give you some idea about the probable behavior of your subject(s). The information from a "lost person questionnaire" will give you very important information as to how your subject may interpret or "see" the environment in your assigned search segment.

A quick way to discriminate relevant clues is by "aging." What we mean by aging is that a searcher should be able to judge how long the suspected clue has been in the environment. For example, if the subject was known to enjoy a particular brand of soft drink, you would, of course, "key" on that particular soft drink container in the search area. Unfortunately, due to the commonplace occurrence of littering, you might find several clues which match that description. Clue items which have been discarded far earlier than the subject was reported missing can be ignored as irrelevant clues (but, it's not a bad idea to pick up trash for the sake of the environment!). However, if you are in doubt, assume that the item in question is a relevant clue and treat it in the way you were instructed to handle clues.

OBSERVATIONAL TECHNIQUES

Observation is the mental process of clue seeking. More specifically, observing is the mental process of allowing your mind to accept and to catalog what your eyes are looking at —both what they see directly and peripherally. Observation also includes the acceptance and registration of what your ears hear —that is, actively listening. Observation includes the processing of information from all five of your senses: sight, hearing, smell, taste, and touch.

NIGHTTIME OBSERVATION

Since night searching is extremely important in SAR operations, it is crucial that a searcher understands and is comfortable in the nighttime environment. Nighttime observation will be dependent upon three factors. These factors are the amount of natural lighting, the intensity of artificial lighting, and the terrain and vegetation in your search area.

NATURAL LIGHTING

The primary source of natural lighting at night is **moonlight**. The amount of light we receive from the moon varies directly with its phase. By phase we mean whether it is a full moon (2nd quarter phase), a three- quarter moon (a gibbous moon), a half moon (1st & 3rd quarter phase), a quarter moon (a crescent moon), or a new moon (4th quarter phase.

Since moonlight is really sunlight reflected off of the rough and dusty lunar surface, the light we receive from a full moon is less than 1/400,000 as much light as we receive from the sun. But a full moon on a clear night is bright enough to produce shadows. How pronounced the shadowing will depend upon the time of the year and on the time at night. The lower the moon is to the horizon, the longer the shadows become and the more pronounced the terrain becomes. The higher the moon, the less will be the shadowing. This combination of "dark" lighting and shadowing can produce optical illusions. Depth and shapes can become extremely distorted. You should keep this in mind during nighttime travel and searching. Shadowing can "black out", that is, shroud portions of the area to your view. Therefore, you will have to concentrate your flashlight beams into these areas more often for more, effective nighttime searching.

When a full moon (or even a gibbous moon) is above an overcast sky of cloud cover, the quality of the light becomes scattered and unable to cast shadows. The natural light becomes diffused and the light becomes more evenly scattered throughout the sky and produces an overall nighttime "glow" to the overall sky and environment. This condition can, in many cases, provide even better light than a clear night sky. There are less optical illusions to contend with and several areas will not become "blackened" due to shadowing.

Half moon (1st & 3rd quarters) light is 10% of full moonlight. A half moon can still be somewhat useful on a search during clear or a lightly overcast sky. However, a crescent moon will provide very little light for the human eye. Users of starlight-scopes, on the other hand, may find that a crescent moon is quite useful.

It may come as a surprise to some, but nighttime travel through forested areas without flashlights during a full moon is quite easy. One can see well enough to navigate cross-country and can search for relatively large clues at long ranges (beyond 15 meters). Exposure to white light will not wash out night vision as much as it would during darker conditions.

Another somewhat steady (although off and on), natural source of light at night is from **auroras**. The Aurora Borealis occurs in the northern hemisphere, the "Northern Lights". The Aurora Australis occurs in the southern hemisphere, the "Southern Lights". The auroras are high-altitude, multicolored lights produced by high-energy particles. This phenomena occurs at high altitudes (usually between 80 to 160 km) over the higher latitudes above the polar regions. The Northern Lights have been seen as far south as Florida. However, the brightest illumination will occur at the higher latitudes.

Starlight is another natural source of light. However, it does not provide enough light for the naked human eye to see well. However, users of starlight-scopes will find that starlight is quite useful.

Lightning is a transient light source. Lightning provides very short bursts of illumination. This type of natural lighting is useful only if you happen to be looking at just the right place or catch something in your peripheral vision.

Nocturnal Visual Effects during nighttime observation presents some unique optical effects. Bright colors will be lost because the rods (the dark visual sensors of the retina's of your eyes) only respond to dim light for black-white vision. These rods reside in the peripherals of our vision. Therefore you will be able to see objects better in your peripheral vision than in your direct vision in a dark environment. You can observe this effect at night by looking directly at a dimly-lit star. Once you've picked out a star,

Chapter 7 - Search Techniques and Tactics

look off to one side or the other and notice what happens. The star will appear to become "brighter" as you move your sight from "on the star" to "off of the star".

Another effect is that terrain can easily be **"washed out"** at night. This effect is particularly pronounced in the desert. In fact, it can pose a serious danger in areas with cliffs and short drop-offs. This wash out effect occurs because of the eye's loss of visual acuity in dimly lit conditions. Darkness will modify outlines, shapes, and coloration of nearby objects. It will also distort distances whereby making dark- colored objects appear further away and light-colored objects appear closer than they really are. Soviet Army studies indicate that on a clear night, an individual can recognize land relief and coloration up to 400 meters. Under a full moon, at high elevation, one can spot a man moving at 240 meters and at 700 meters if binoculars are used. These distances assume sufficient background contrast.

Vertigo (dizziness) can occur during snow storms. It happens most often when the searcher holds a very bright flashlight in a high position and walks briskly. Possible solutions to this problem are to switch to a less intense light and/or to mount the light lower to the ground, perhaps on a tracking stick. Also, it helps to switching the flashlight lens from clear to an amber color.

ARTIFICIAL LIGHTING

Artificial light includes any type of illumination you might carry with you into the search environment. Head lamps are excellent for searching on and just off a trail. They provide "hands-free" searching. However, most head lamps are not powerful enough to beam further than 15 meters. A possible solution is to carry a "caving-type" of head lamp; one which has a powerful, but controllable beam and powered by a large battery pack.

Another excellent artificial light source are the professional type of large flashlights which utilize aircraft-quality aluminum for their construction and exotic types of bulbs. The flashlights which use 3 or more size 'D' alkaline cell batteries connected in series work the best. The lens can be focused in a way that spreads the beam's "footprint" over a large area appropriate to close and medium range searches. Or, you can focus a narrow beam to illuminate areas well beyond 15 meters. The drawback is the size and weight of these types of lights. Also, be wary of the rechargeable variety of these flashlights because they lose their charge rapidly and the batteries cannot be recharged while on the move. There are endless versions of portable lighting devices available and you should experiment to find the right system for your own needs.

Another consideration is the use of colored filters. It is very useful to have one or more colored filters for your flashlights. White light "bleaches out" your night vision whereas red light will provide illumination without the bleaching of night vision. Amber lenses are good to use in fog and/or vertigo-type conditions. Green lenses are good for reading fine print on a map at night.

Some final recommendations are that each searcher should carry at the minimum two sources of light. It is highly recommended that you carry three sources of light, and have light hardware whose parts are interchangeable. That way you can almost always maintain a light source. It is good to carry one high powered light, and a few others as backups, for map reading or other utility tasks.

TERRAIN AND VEGETATION

The terrain can effect nighttime observation. The more technical (steep) the terrain becomes, the more difficult it becomes to traverse and search. A great amount of vegetation (or a total lack of vegetation) will also effect nighttime observation. Vegetation can hamper both travel and clue seeking.

As was mentioned before, terrain texture becomes washed out at night. This is because your night vision does not provide great visual acuity. At night vegetation can also obscure the terrain. It not only conceals clues, but can also camouflage abrupt terrain changes. Therefore, if searchers are to search areas off routes at night, it is imperative to have good quality flashlights and to avoid relying solely on natural lighting.

Some **special precautions** are needed for a night search. These include being very aware of "tanglefoot." Tanglefoot is any material which catches your feet when you walk, thus causing you to trip and perhaps injure yourself. Tanglefoot includes brush, stumps, and any abrupt change in the terrain. Such a hazard unfortunately forces a searcher to focus more attention on traveling than on clue seeking. One very good solution is to use teamwork. Have the point-person focus on what's ahead on the ground calling out upcoming hazards (or clues). The other crew members can then follow the point and handle the majority of searching off the route as well as perform other crew duties such as navigation.

Another, very serious danger on night searches is **eye hazards.** These would include sticker bushes, branches and anything else hanging at eye-level. Such hazards can result in a range of problems from mere nuisance to very serious eye damage. One way to protect yourself is to wear glasses instead of contact lens. People who don't wear eyeglasses can wear clear industrial safety glasses during night searches. As with tanglefoot, you could have the point person call out hazards at eye level as well as on the ground. Avoiding crew injuries will certainly improve the crew's search effectiveness.

IMPROVING OBSERVATIONAL TECHNIQUES

The way to improve observation technique is to practice. And, practicing in your primary response area in all sorts of conditions is the best way to improve your observation skills. If you can't get out into the woods, you can practice being observant while taking walks through your own neighborhood. The important thing is learn to be an *active* observer.

How well you observe will be highly dependent upon your training and experience. If your training and experience has been in the flat fields of farm country, then your observational skills will not be highly developed in heavy forest with lots of ridges and ravines. Therefore, the environment in which you conduct your training will greatly effect your ability to search in that same type of environment.

Your personal conditioning will be a factor in your effectiveness. Such factors as your health, physical condition, nutrition, hydration, rest, stress, attitude, morale, and discipline will all play an important role. If you are not conditioned for the search environment, you will not be effective as a searcher.

Your knowledge of the search subject(s) and situation will greatly influence your capacity to observe. You will need to know *exactly what* you are looking for in order to be effective. Spend some time between search assignments to review subject information updates that may be available.

Keep in mind that even though we will concentrate our discussion on visual clue seeking, it is important that you pay attention to what your other senses are also telling you. Thus, use your sense of hearing and smell as you search.

SCANNING *VS.* OBSERVING

Scanning is the *physical process* of moving your eyes, head, and body to effectively observe the surrounding environment for clues. **Observing** is the *mental process* of clue seeking. They are separate processes, but they are synergistic too. It is important to understand that scanning and observing are component parts to clue seeking. You can literally walk through a clue "enriched" environment and make all the motions of moving your head from left to right, but miss several clues because you were scanning without observing. Therefore, you must learn to combine these two sets of skills to be an effective searcher.

THE PHYSICS OF LIGHT

It is important to understand some of the basic physics of how light behaves and the physiology of human vision. Knowing such behavior will better equip you for both day and night searching. But, before we discuss "how" we see, we will examine some of the ways that light can interact with the environment. We will examine three ways that light interacts with the environment. These three are *reflection, refraction,* and *diffraction*.

Reflected light is light which bounces off a surface. The angle at which it reflects off of the surface is identical to the same angle by which it strikes the surface. Light gently reflected from snow can be very helpful at night because it tends to fill in shadowed areas. On the other hand, during daytime, intense light reflected off snow can "white out" a searcher's vision if he/she doesn't have adequate eye protection.

Refracted light is light which becomes bent from passing through materials of different optical densities. This effect occurs in the atmosphere when the moon or the sun is low in the sky. Their size appears larger and their usual colors become distorted as they approach the horizon. This same effect is also noted on land while looking for clues which are submerged under the water's surface. Submerged objects appear distorted in size and location. For instance a coin in shallow water looks larger and closer to the surface than it really is. Fishing line appears to bend at the surface where the medium of air meets the medium of water.

Diffracted light bends around obstacles in its way. This phenomena is responsible for the "diffused light" effect that occurs with an overcast sky. The light becomes diffused as it passes around water molecules in the atmosphere. This effect provides the "glow" to the search environment on nights with a bright moon and medium to lightly overcast skies.

THE PHYSIOLOGY OF VISION

The average human eye is sensitive to a range of light frequencies between about 700 nanometers (red light) to about 400 nanometers (violet light). We call this range "visible light." At the center of this spectrum, at 550 nanometers, is green light. It is at this frequency that the eye is most sensitive. The sensitivity to light drops off quickly when light frequencies depart from this median frequency. The eye perceives light via two types of photoreceptors found on the back inside surface of the eyeball. These receptors, known as *cones* and *rods*, reside in a area which we call the retina.

Cones are one type of photoreceptor within the eye. They number about 7 million per eye. Cones provide daylight color vision and are responsible for visual acuity (sharpness). The majority of cones are concentrated in the central portion of the eye's visual field. It is this portion of the eye which will "see" objects during daytime. We call this our "day vision". Cones come in three types: red, green and blue. Each type responds to a range of related light frequencies. When the brain combines the data coming from the three types of cones we see the full spectrum of colors.

In addition to the cones, the typical human eye contains 100 million rods. Rods are the photoreceptors which are responsive to dim light for black and white vision. The majority are positioned in the peripheral parts of the eye. Rods can detect form and movement but they provide relatively poor visual acuity. It is this portion of the eye, the periphery, which will "see" objects during very dark conditions. Rods are far more sensitive to light than cones. The ability to see during very dim lighting conditions is called "night vision."

During daylight, the rods are over stimulated and their visual response is "washed-out". Therefore, the cones provide the majority of daylight vision. On the other hand, the cones' comparatively low sensitivity provides us with excellent visual acuity during bright conditions.

Night vision, or perhaps more precisely, "dark adaptation" will take about 20 to 30 minutes to fully develop. This is the time it takes for rods to fully "recharge" their responsive pigment. Vitamin "A" is a necessary nutrient for this chemical reaction to occur. But once night vision has been established it can be easily neutralized if the eye is exposed to strong white light which overwhelms the rods causing night vision to be "bleached out." Red light, however, is not absorbed by the rods and does not bleach them out and therefore red light leaves night vision in tact. Under red light the red cones are also stimulated and they help to provide some visual acuity even on the darkest of nights. Therefore, be careful about flashing white light in the eyes of fellow searchers. You may wish to use a red colored lens on your "map light" for reading maps and operations orders at night.

Even though red light is best at sparing night vision, the human eye can see green colored objects at night easier than red colored objects. This is because red light is not absorbed well by the red cones pigment. Green light is better absorbed than red. If light isn't absorbed it can't produce the photochemical reaction responsible for vision.

The small area where the optic nerve attaches to the back of the eye is known as the *optical disc*. This area consists purely of nerves. With neither rods nor cones, the optical disk is literally our "blind spot." Because of the eye's constant movement, we are usually unaware of the blind spot. With both eyes open, objects are viewed at two different angles, thus providing binocular (and stereoscopic) vision. The brain automatically fills in the blind spot because it remembers what it saw on a previous pass of your eyes. So, if you keep your eyes or angle of vision moving, you will be able to compensate for the blind spot.

SCANNING RANGES

The eyes are unable to focus at two distances at one time. For this reason we divide our scanning into three ranges that go from that which is immediately before our eyes to that which approaches the horizon. But regardless of which range you are actively observing, you must always keep in mind that your chance of seeing a clue will be greater if you make short stops and to allow your eyes to briefly refocus. Merely sliding your vision over an area quickly without pausing will not guarantee you will see what you are looking at. Pausing to focus between scans will give you the best chance of sighting a clue.

SHORT RANGES (WITHIN ONE METER)

This closest scanning range includes looking for clues within one meter (3.28 feet) from your eyes. It is mostly used during tracking operations by the point-person. Just as in tracking, during short range scanning you need to key on outlines, shapes, contrasts, colors and movement. Try to use a regular scanning pattern. This will ensure a greater chance at detecting a clue.

MEDIUM RANGES (BETWEEN 1 TO 15 METERS)

This middle scanning range includes looking for clues from one meter (3.28 feet) up to fifteen meters (49.2 feet) from your eyes. This middle range is usually used by hasty, efficient and thorough search tactics.

LONG RANGES (BEYOND 15 METERS)

This long scanning range includes looking for clues beyond fifteen meters (49.2 feet) from your eyes. It is mostly used in hasty and efficient search tactics.

As in the middle range, we look for clues keying on outlines, shapes, contrasts, colors and movement. We prefer to use the "breakup" scan technique to maximize the amount of information the brain can process.

BREAKUP SCANNING PROCEDURE

The "breakup" scanning procedure is one type of scanning procedure that you may wish to use on medium and long range scans. It requires you to mentally "breakup" your search area into separate arcs or sectors or quadrants to be scanned. You then scan each arc separately in a systematic process. The reason for this is so that you will maximize the probability that you will detect a clue. It also helps to ensure that each sector has been scanned and nothing has been ignored.

Instead of sweeping your eyes across an entire 180 degree arc, break up the full 180 degree arc into four 45 degree segments. Take the first arc, sweeping back and forth slowly while pausing every 10 degrees or so. Then do a second arc at a greater distance, sweep back & forth segment by segment. This technique will force you to scan aggressively, but it will also help you to scan thoroughly and carefully! You could use the breakup scan method for an arc in front of you or one that is off to your side. You may even use it in a 360 degree sweep. No matter

Chapter 7 - Search Techniques and Tactics

how you decide to break up an arc to be scanned (30-45-60-90 degrees), try to train yourself to consistently scan in a routine and disciplined fashion. But remember, if your scan is too large, your effectiveness will decrease and you will be prone to miss a clue. If your scan arc is too small, you will fatigue faster and your efficiency will decrease.

BACK SCANNING

Research has shown that 56% of the clues can be found by simply looking behind one's self. Therefore, "back scanning" should certainly become part of your scanning pattern. In the case of hasty crew searching during which an area is searched by two crew members in tandem, it would be beneficial to assign one crew member to perform the majority of the back scanning.

NIGHTTIME SCANNING

Because of the physiology of our eyes, the key to nighttime scanning is to move your central focus to 5 degrees off of the intended area so that the visual rods are used to their best advantage. The "figure-8" method is most effective. Move your scan in a figure-8 pattern in the direction of the area to be searched. Be sure to use short, abrupt, darting movements as you do. Pause at each short stop. However, do not allow your pause to linger for more than a few seconds because if you pause too long any object will begin to blend in with the background.

IMPROVING SCANNING TECHNIQUES

As with improving your observation techniques, the best way for you to improve your scanning technique is simply to practice. Ideally, practicing in your primary response area in all types of conditions is best. But, even if you can't get into your search environment to practice, you can practice while you take walks through your own neighborhood, and that's better than not practicing at all. Therefore, actively train yourself to do active scanning. It will become so automatic that you won't even have to think about it.

SCAN QUADRANTS

The term that defines a 90 degree arc is a "quadrant." (360 degrees divided by 4 = 90 degrees.)

The 1st quadrant is the 12 to 3 O'clock position relative to the searcher. The 2nd quadrant is the 3 to 6 O'clock position of the searcher. The 3rd quadrant is the 6 to 9 O'clock position of the searcher. The 4th quadrant is the 9 to 12 O'clock position of the searcher.

CRITICAL SPACING

Critical Spacing (or Critical Separation) is an "elastic unit" which overcomes the problems associated with varying terrain, visibility, weather, and scan-distance of the individual searchers. Critical Spacing (CS) optimizes the distance between searchers so that efficiency is not sacrificed for effectiveness.

In some respects, critical spacing can be thought of as a "refinement" in an efficient search. In the past, the problem facing many SAR managers and crews was to determine what spacing distances should be assigned to a crew on a sweep. Crews were assigned distances based on standardized charts, but those charts only applied to a certain 'standard' terrain with a 'standard' type of vegetation. Those early POD charts did not take into consideration the many variables such as size of clues and natural light conditions.

The theory of Critical Spacing (CS) takes into consideration the distance at which a searcher can identify a certain sized clue under the then-existing environmental conditions. These conditions include the terrain, vegetation, and the natural and/or artificial lighting. Critical spacing can be determined by using what is known as the "Norththumberland Raindance". The following is an algorithm to determine CS:

• Place an object on the ground representing the smallest size of the clues you wish to key on. Be sure to do this outside in the same environment that you will be doing your search.

- Then, you and your crew should walk around the object while you slowly expand your distance from the object.
- Once you reach the distance at which the object can barely be seen, stop!
- Then determine your distance to the object via tally step. That distance becomes your personal critical "sighting".
- Everyone in the crew will no doubt have his/her own personal critical sighting distance. A low average of those distances will determine the distance that should be used for the crew's critical sighting distance.
- When you double this sighting distance, you have determined the crew's Critical Spacing or Separation because each person can see half way to the next person on the line.

For example, if you and your crew average your critical sighting range at 30 meters, then twice that number, 60 meters, would be your crew's critical spacing. In other words, each member of your search crew would space themselves at a distance of 60 meters on the base line before you start your sweep. This would be the greatest range at which two searchers could just see the size of clues you are trying to find in the type of environment you are in.

For a numerical expression of CS, critical spacing is assigned the factor of "1.0". Distances which are greater than CS are assigned numbers greater than 1. Distances which are less than CS are assigned numbers less than 1. A perfect CS = 1 will yield a probability of detection of 50%. As the separation increases, the POD decreases, thus a loss of effectiveness. Conversely, as the distance decreases, the POD increases, but at a cost of efficiency. To better illustrate this concept, please note "Searcher Spacing verses POD" by Dave Perkins of Northumberland National Park, UK.

- At a CS of 1, the POD is 50%.
- At a CS of 2 the POD is 25%.
- At a CS of 0.5 the POD is 75%.

VISUAL CS
Critical spacing can be determined by visual methods by using what has been called the "Norththumberland Raindance". It is suggested that a navigator be assigned at the center position of the sweep. You would then assign two flankers; one to each side of the navigator. The flankers should space themselves out at a distance from the navigator at slightly below critical spacing. This will ensure navigational control while allowing for the flankers to concentrate on the majority of the searching. Thus, teamwork is applied to the search.

VOCAL CS
Critical spacing could also be determined vocally. This technique will ensure that searchers are always within hearing range of the subject's calls. This is useful when searching for responsive subjects who call to the searchers.

STOP-SPIN-SCAN
This technique should be applied with any type of sweep operation. Stop-Spin-Scan (SSS) means to *stop* every distance at one-half of the critical separation, turn completely around (*spin*) to carefully and deliberately look around, so the searcher can *scan* the surrounding area for the subject or for clues. This technique ensures a positive search effort. Research has demonstrated that over one-half of clues could have been found by simply looking behind oneself. Dave Perkins recommends that this SSS procedure should occur at intervals of ½ the CS distance. Therefore if CS = 100 feet, each member of the line should stop to SSS each 50 feet they advance.

PURPOSEFUL WANDERING
It is not expected that the searchers on a sweep will blindly march along in a straight line. They will be "wandering purposefully" scanning and observing the environment for clues. The important thing is for each crew member to keep track of the line he/she is supposed to walk and to maintain roughly the correct CS distance between the crew member to the left and to the right.

As we have said, in theory, CS at 1.0 will yield a POD of 50%. However, with the enhanced combination of Stop-Spin-Scan and Purposeful Wandering, and maintaining the CS distance, your crews will increase the POD dramatically to 80%!

SEARCH TACTICS

SEARCH OVERVIEW

The following is a review of various search tactics. Passive tactics are those that do not require searchers to actively go out to find clues or the lost subject. Active tactics include those which do require searchers to actively go find clues and the lost subject.

PASSIVE TACTICS

Fact finding tactics includes tactics such as interviewing the last person who saw the lost subject or the family members of the lost subject. Searchers need to know as much about the subject as possible so that clues found during the search have meaning. If you know something about the victim, you will be in a position to ask questions of the people you may meet while you are searching for him/her. Never pass by a hiker without politely asking for information of what they have seen or heard. They often will have clues, which will only make sense when you piece together their information with information you have about the victim.

And occasionally, the "hiker" himself has been found to be the subject of the search! Investigation into the lost subject's background is also considered to be a fact finding method of passive search tactics.

Attraction tactics use visual devices (red lights on an emergency vehicle) or audible devices (loud speakers) to bring the lost subject to a specific location. These tactics help the subject find the searchers.

Confinement tactics which may be used to limit the lost subject's movement include track traps, trail blocks, or road blocks.

Electronic search equipment tactics such as the use of listening devices, night vision scopes, electronic locator receivers are becoming more useful in finding the lost subject.

Active tactics include:

- Class I-Criterion is <u>Speed</u>, Commonly called Hasty Searching
- Class II-Criterion is <u>Efficiency</u>
- Class III-Criterion is <u>Thoroughness</u>

SEARCH DETECTION MAXIMIZATION

The object is to, as quickly as possible, locate clues which may eventually lead to the lost subject. How quick and how well those clues are found will greatly depend on the training and experience of the search crews. A crew needs to maximize its search detection capabilities. This is not to say that they must plod along at a very slow rate and in the process turn over every rock and twig! However, they must be able to consistently scan for important clues while traversing vast areas.

SEARCH CREW TACTICS

We define search "tactics" as the teamwork procedures which are used by a search crew or team to solve a search problem. In other words, tactics are the collective skills brought together in teamwork fashion to seek out clues and search for subjects. In addition, tactics are used by a search crew or team to carry out the planned strategy of searching an area.

The goal of search tactics is to systematically guide trained clue seekers (searchers) through probable search areas. Search tactics can be divided into two major categories; the first of which is passive tactics and the second is active tactics. As was briefly discussed in the Introduction to this section, tactics can take on a variety of forms. In this text we will not examine in detail all tactics used by SAR personnel. We will, however, examine tactics used by foot-based searchers and dog handlers. Even though we focus primarily on land search tactics, some of these tactics are universal to all search environments and with all types of transportation capabilities.

We will first examine what some call the "types" or "classes" of active search. We would prefer to call them "classes" of searches because of possible confusion between types of resources and types of searches.

The *first class* "Hasty" is a fast search primarily looking for the subject. The *second class* "Efficient" is more systematic and will usually be slower than the first. The *third class* "Thorough" is highly systematic and is very time consuming and manpower intensive.

In addition, we will introduce some refinements to "Hasty" and "Efficient" tactics. We will also look at special tactics using tracking skills. Finally, we will review some confinement search tactics.

HASTY SEARCH
(route or segment)

Hasty Search or "Class I" is a fast tactic which uses small, highly trained crews to find subjects or major clues in the quickest possible way. It can also be used to examine areas which hold little potential for finding the subject. The earlier term for this level of search was "Type I". The term "type" is an ICS (Incident Command System) designation that describes the capability of the searcher, as opposed to the kind of search the searcher is doing.

As the name "Hasty" implies, this tactic is done as swiftly as possible. The mission of the hasty crew is to search, move, and communicate. This tactic may use foot-based searchers, dogs and handlers, aircraft, landcraft, or watercraft. The emphasis is upon **speed**. The hasty crew must briskly search for the subject(s) through several areas or for initial clues upon which the remainder of the search will be based. A lack of clues is in itself a clue and can be just as important as finding a clue. A lack of clues may indicate the necessity of redirecting the searchers. A hasty search can take place in two separate areas at the same time. For example, one crew might search along a route and another crew through an off-route area.

A **route search** requires the crew to follow either a man-made route or a natural land form route as its guide. This type of search can yield excellent results. Historical data shows the many lost subjects will attempt to stay on some sort of route as opposed to wandering aimlessly. Routes which are well traveled may yield important clues in so-called **track-trap** areas. Navigation is somewhat easier in a **route search** than in an **area search**. If the route is depicted on the search map, then the crew can keep track of its location by using the route as a navigational "handrail".

Examples of routes include:
- Roads
- Trails and minor footpaths
- Ridgelines
- Relatively small, confined valleys, natural or man-made drainages
- Hazardous areas
- Natural or man-made refuges (caves, caverns, overhangs, buildings, tunnels, etc.)
- Game trails

An **area search** requires the crew to use an artificial navigational device (such as a compass) to guide its direction. An open area will usually not, itself, be a route, but the open area may cut across several natural routes which were made geologically or by animals. Accomplishing the assignment will require the crew to use fundamental map and compass skills, as well as skills for determining distances.

TYPES OF RESOURCES USED FOR HASTY SEARCHES

Hasty crews need to be very agile and mobile. Their searching techniques must also be very aggressive. The crew must be able to travel quickly through the area and must be able to search while on the move. Fixed and rotary-winged aircraft are good resources in Hasty Searches. In addition, 4X4 vehicles and boats can provide rapid travel to and through the search area.

Trails and back country areas most often require foot travel, however, it may be possible to utilize all-terrain vehicles (ATV), mountain bikes or horses for rapid transport. An important consideration when employing mountain bikes and horses is to be sure to brief the crews to be careful not to destroy clues on a trail. In addition, bike crews need to understand the importance of making frequent stops to scan 360 degrees. A bike rider on the move in the back country will be more apt to focus on the route ahead of him/herself than to search the surrounding area.

HASTY SEARCH CREW FORMATIONS

The following formations refer primarily to foot-based search methods. There are additional formations which some units have used successfully in search, but we will only examine the most basic formations. A typical hasty crew consists of between 2 and 3 searchers but may have more members if applicable. A rule of thumb is that the smaller the crew, the faster it will travel.

SINGLE FILE FORMATION

This is the most fundamental formation. The lead individual, is known as the "point,". The point might be assigned as the navigator or simply a searcher. The crewleader usually follows the point. The other crew member follows in file. Each member scans left and right with the last member scanning periodically to the rear. This method is mostly used for hasty searching along routes or for the purpose of traveling quickly to areas of high probability.

Scan Ranges: Medium to Long

Advantages: Very fast moving. Good for finding obvious clues right upon or just off of the route.

Disadvantages: Covers a very small area. Easy to inadvertently miss or destroy clues on the route.

SWEEP FORMATION

This type of formation requires the searchers to spread out abreast of one another to form

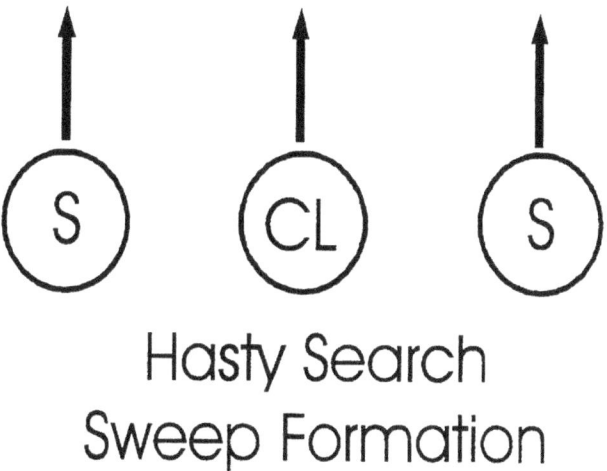

Figure 7.2

a line. This formation may be required to search through areas quickly, using wide spacing.

Most Used For: Hasty searching large areas, also used for searching along the side of a particular route.

Scan Ranges: Medium to Long.

Advantages: Fast moving. Covers a wide area along a trail or though a segment.

Disadvantages: It tends to move slower than a single file formation. Speed depends greatly upon the crew's experience and the local environment.

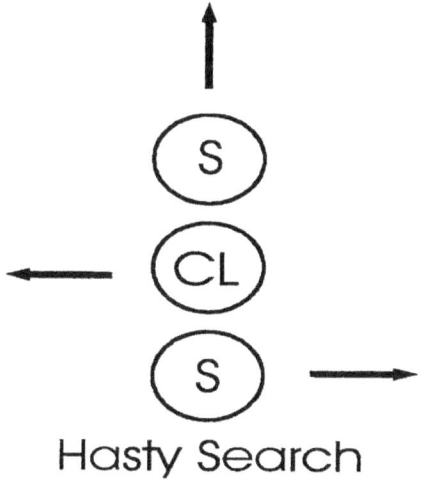

Figure 7.1

CREW DUTIES AND ASSIGNMENTS

Each crew member should be assigned a specific duty such as navigation (azimuth and/or tally) or radio operator or crewleader. In addition, each crew member should be assigned a particular quadrant or side to search. These assignments will ensure maximum coverage and minimize redundancy.

For example, a three-member hasty crew traveling in a single file formation along a route could be assigned as follows. The crewleader assigns himself/herself the responsibility for navigation using a compass, map and terrain analysis and scan left and right. Another member is assigned the point position. He/she scans the trail to the front and sides, looks for hazards, and leads the crew to their assigned destination. The last crew member is assigned to monitor his/her tally steps; monitor the radio; and scans left, right and to the rear every ten tally steps.

The crew, using coordinated teamwork, travels briskly to their assigned destination while ensuring that all four quadrants are being scanned for the subject or for clues. It is strongly recommended that crew assignments be made before the crew departs on its search mission. Without specific assignments for each searcher, searchers may fall victim to the "follow the leader" mentality or they may watch the back of each others packs rather than look for the subject.

EFFICIENT SEARCH

Efficient Search or "Class II" is a relatively fast, systematic tactic which uses small but highly trained crews to search segments using "critical spacing" or greater. It is another method used to search large areas with small numbers of resources. Like hasty search tactics, efficient search tactics focuses on time not thoroughness.

The efficient search tactic has recently been refined by employing the concept of "critical separation" or "critical spacing" that was developed by members of the Northumberland National Park, UK.

TYPES OF RESOURCES USED FOR EFFICIENT SEARCHES

A typical efficient crew can consist of between 3 to 5 searchers but may have more members if applicable. This type of tactic should only be attempted by individuals who are trained and who can maintain spacing control.

EFFICIENT SEARCH CREW FORMATIONS

There are two basic types of efficient search formations. The first is the **Sweep** formation. It is similar to the sweep formation we discussed in the hasty search technique section. Each crew member is lined up perpendicular to the direction of the sweep. Each crew member strives to maintain a rough distance from each other while traversing the area for clues.

The line at which the crew lines up in preparation to performing a sweep is called the "Base Line." As the crew is sweeping the area, it utilizes some form of "Control Line" to maintain a heading. This control line may be an object to guide (such as a road) or a magnetic compass azimuth.

If, for example, we have five crew members sweeping along the side of a road off to the right side (guiding to their left). The interval between searchers might be 40 meters. This search would be known as, **5 - Guide Left along road - 40 meters.**

If, for example, we had three crew members sweeping through a forest on a magnetic azimuth of 280 degrees, and they were separated at an interval of 50 meters between each searcher, we would designate this search as, **3 - Compass 280 - 50 meters.**

The second type of efficient search formation is the **Wedge**. The wedge is similar to the sweep with the exception of the "guide person" who is at a flanker position and is slightly ahead (one to five meters) of the adjacent searcher. Each adjacent searcher is slightly behind and guides off of the searcher next to him/her. This type of formation may result in better spacing control than the sweep, especially during nighttime search operations. There will be less chance of "flashing" a searcher's eyes with a light beam and thus disabling his/her night vision.

Chapter 7 - Search Techniques and Tactics

EFFICIENT SEARCH CREW SPACING

Wide Spacing Line Searches are those in which the interval between searchers is 30 meters or greater (or beyond about 100 feet). This type of spacing is also termed "open line search". One technique used in efficient search methods is "Critical Spacing". Critical Spacing is indicated by "CS"

Spacing with CS = 1. By definition, CS = 1 is spacing at the designated critical spacing. For example, if CS was determined to be 30 meters, we would say the CS = 1 at 30 meters. And at CS the POD would be 50%. If these same searchers were to add "purposeful wandering" to their search technique, the POD could be increased to about 80% at CS = 1. **(See Figure 7.3)**

Spacing with CS > 1. These are spacings greater than the designated critical spacing. For example, if CS for a given situation was determined to be 50 meters, then any distance beyond 50 meters would be considered greater than one CS In that case we would say CS = 1 at 50 meters, therefore CS = 2 at 100 meters. This is an important concept because as the distance increases beyond critical spacing the POD (Probability of Detection) decreases. **(See Figure 7.4)**

Spacing with CS < 1. These are spacings less than the designated critical spacing. For example, if CS was determined to be 30 meters, then any distance less than 30 meters would be considered something less than CS. Therefore, if

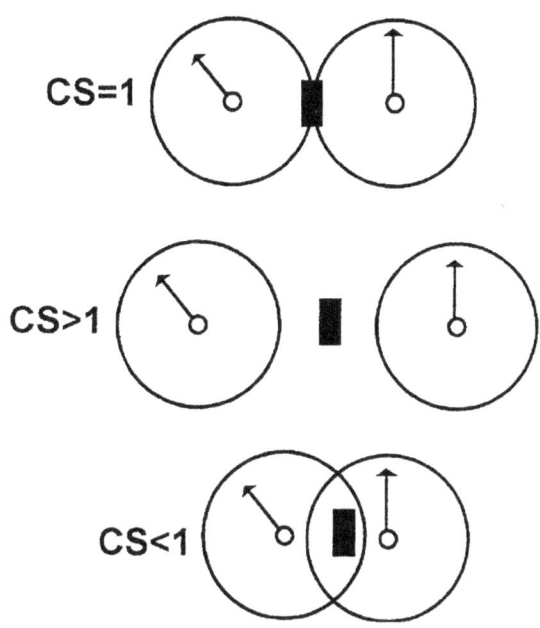

Figure 7.4

CS = 1 at 30 meters then CS = 0.5 at 15 meters. As the CS decreases, the POD increases. In this example the POD at 15 meters would be 75%.

CREW DUTIES AND ASSIGNMENTS

Crew duties may be assigned similar to what we described when we talked about the hasty crews. The difference in the Efficient Search is each searcher on the sweep line is responsible for searching all four quadrants within his/her immediate area.

THOROUGH SEARCH

The Thorough Search or "Class III" is a slow, highly systematic search which utilizes large, semi-trained crews to sweep search areas. The Thorough Search class has been called "grid search" in the past. The Thorough Search maybe used to effectively search small areas. Typical crew member spacings are far below "critical spacing". It should be used only as a last resort or for evidence searches. It is very inefficient and requires great numbers of personnel.

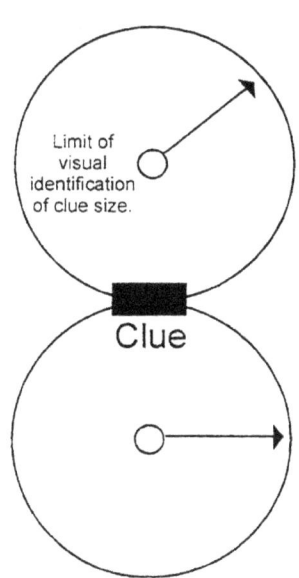

Figure 7.3

TYPES OF RESOURCES USED FOR THOROUGH SEARCHES

A typical thorough search crew will consist of between 5 to 10 searchers but may have more members if applicable. This type of tactic can be employed using people who are trained or semi-trained but they must be able to maintain spacing control.

THOROUGH SEARCH CREW FORMATIONS

The same sweep and wedge formations used in the efficient search could be utilized in the thorough search.

THOROUGH SEARCH CREW SPACING

Close Spacing Line Searches (Less than 100 feet) Close spacing is considered to be searcher-to-searcher separations of less than 100 feet (or within about 30 meters). This type of spacing is also termed "closed line search" or "grid search". It is almost always used with a CS<1.

CREW DUTIES AND ASSIGNMENTS

Crew duties may be assigned similar to what we described in hasty and efficient crew searches. It will usually be necessary to assign two individuals on the search line to handle navigation duties, especially when large numbers of searchers are involved.

SIGNCUTTING TACTICS

Signcutting tactics are considered to be an Efficient Search but because of the amount of information about this topic we have listed it separately. Signcutting tactics use tracking techniques to search for signs in order to initiate a Step-by-Step tracking operation. It is assumed that the reader already has some familiarity with both tracking and signcutting. What will be discussed in this next section will build upon what the student has already learned in a NASAR Fundamentals of Search and Rescue (FUNSAR) course. It will give you some ideas about how to apply effective signcutting tactics to a variety of search situations.

SIGNCUTTING FORMATION

This type of formation requires the searchers to use a CS=1 or less in a line formation. This differs from the Step-by-Step tracking formation, which is an inverted "V" or "Wishbone" formation. This type of formation is most advantageous for a signcutting operation because each person is looking for any possible sign of the lost subject. The members concentrate their attention for about one to two meters looking for small signs to the front, left and right. They also must scan the four quadrants for large signs or converging and diverging tracks.

Most Used For: Signcutting along suspected routes, perpendicular across the subject direction of travel, around the location of a known clue or through areas containing track traps.

Scan Ranges: Short to Medium.

Advantages: Can determine the direction of travel of the subject. Requires small numbers of resources.

Disadvantages: Slower than Hasty Search tactics, requires highly trained personnel.

SIGNCUTTING A PLS OR AN LKP

At the start of every search operation, every effort should be made to signcut around the place-last-seen (PLS) or the last-known-point (LKP). This technique can give you both the direction-of-travel and help you to (initially) eliminate potential search segments.

Initially, the signcutting crew should scan the general vicinity for any clues and to get an idea of the condition of the PLS or LKP. It's important to know if the PLS or LKP has been contaminated by people besides the subject(s). The lead signcutter should examine the PLS or LKP for tracks and signs. The crew will then move in a circle around the PLS or LKP. Tracks or sign leaving the PLS or LKP will intersect the circle of the signcut at a 90 degree angle.

If no sign has been discovered by the first circular signcut around the PLS or LKP, carefully increase the circle a few meters further from the PLS or LKP and perform another circular signcut. Continue to repeat this process at a larger radius. If the area has been well trampled by other searchers or other persons, you may need to expand your initial signcut radius.

SIGNCUTTING A ROUTE

If you are assigned to signcut a route, try to keep the route between you and the main source of light (sun at day, flashlight at night). The signcutting crew needs to carefully check trail and route junctions for any sign of direction changes or patches of scuffed up ground where a subject could have stood and shuffled around while trying to decide which side of a fork in the route to take.

SIGNCUTTING PERPENDICULAR TO A SUSPECTED DIRECTION

Perpendicular signcuts to the suspected route of travel of the lost subject are important techniques used in **binary search** strategy. They are used to eliminate potential search segments. The signcut should be made at a 90 degree angle to a suspected direction of travel and well ahead of the LKP. This technique could also be employed even if no direction of travel has been established. It is important to complete the entire signcutting assignment (unless instructed otherwise) to verify whether the subject has maintained or changed their direction of travel.

SIGNCUTTING SUSPECTED SEGMENTS

When you are assigned to signcut a segment, first attempt to cut around the perimeter of the segment. If no sign is found, continue your cut while you spiral cut **inward** towards the central part of the assigned segment.

If the segment is large, consider signcutting the segment in a binary pattern after you have completed the perimeter cut. This means cut the segment roughly in half while looking for sign. If no sign is found, cut each remaining halves into halves and so on. There again, the objective is to eliminate potential search segments so the crew actually searches the most likely areas and avoids the least likely areas.

Excellent places for signcutting within the segment are "Track-Traps". Track-Traps are areas which include stream bottoms, river edges, and any muddy, sandy, or dusty areas. Also, look for any place that would require a person to narrow his path to avoid an obstruction in a trail or path. These obstructions could be a gate, log, rock, or a mud hole. These places can reveal the passage of a lost subject and disclose his/her direction-of-travel.

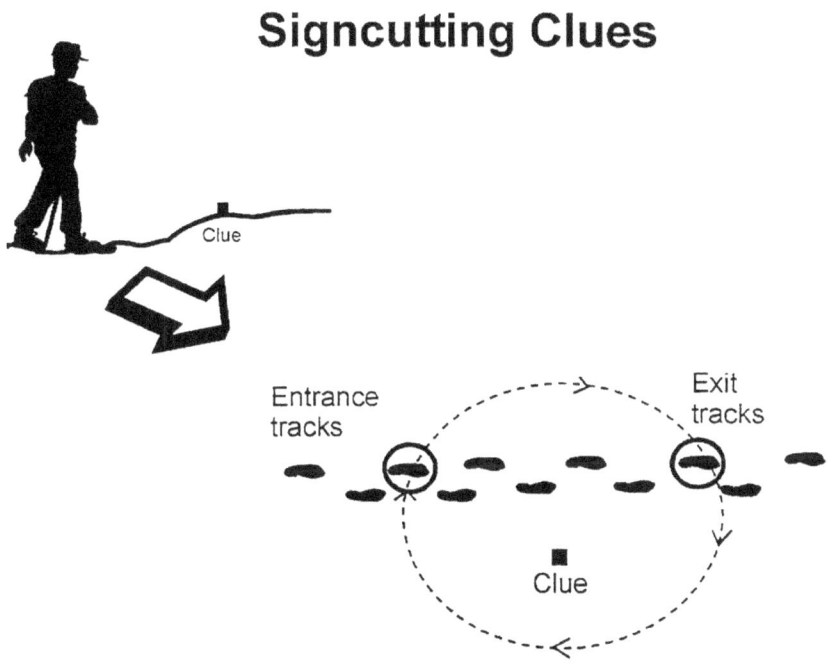

Signcut around each clue found as if LKP

Figure 7.5

SIGNCUTTING AROUND CLUES

Treat all suspected clues as the potential LKP. Preserve the clues as evidence of the subject passing very close to or having been at the clue location. Therefore, as you would do at the

PLS, signcut around each and every clue found to determine the subject's direction of travel. **(See Figure 7.5)**

As you signcut around a suspected clue, be aware that both entry tracks and exit tracks may be present. Just as an EMT inspects gunshot wounds for the entrance and exit of the bullet, you should always inspect the area around a clue for the subject's entry into the area and possible exit from the area.

If tracks or other signs are found, be sure to note the direction of travel (via magnetic azimuth) they indicate. Be sure to record the clue location via UTM coordinates onto your Unit Log. This information will be valuable for the search manager to plan the next strategy.

In addition, be sure to scan the general location to determine if the terrain or vegetation could possibly be "guiding" the subject in a logical direction.

CONFINEMENT TACTICS

Many times confinement tactics include "Passive Tactics" such as trail blocks, lookouts, track traps or listening posts. The confinement tactics also can include patrols by crews or other resources. Signcutting is a common tactic used for confinement when a large number of resources are not available and the terrain is appropriate.

ATTRACTION TACTICS

By far, the easiest attraction device that a search crew can use is the whistle. Calling to the subject works well in the early stages of the search but quickly diminishes as time goes on. If vocal or audible attraction has been used in an area for the first 24 hours without response, it may be determined by the Incident Commander (IC) that such tactics are unlikely to yield a positive response from a subject who may be unable to respond.

SEARCH DOG TACTICS

If, we as Incident Commanders and Search Crewleaders are to accomplish our assigned missions and resolve the Search Operation as efficiently as possible, we should make every effort to use every available resources in our respective areas of Operation. The available resources need to be known by our Planning Section, and the availability of Search Dog Units should be no less important than the other available tools. The key to the most advantageous use of the resources will be in having a working knowledge of the capabilities of each resource and at what point its use will contribute to a successful outcome. Search Dogs Units have been operating for several decades. They have enjoyed great success in resolving complicated search missions over extremely difficult terrain. This section is intended to acquaint you with Search Dogs Units, how they operate, and how to use them to your best advantage.

A dog's ability to detect scent and determine the subject's direction of travel defies scientific measurement. A well-trained scent dog can detect and recognize a scent at a concentration of less than 1:1,000,000,000,000 (1 part in 1 trillion). Scenting dogs have located gas line leaks that were undetectable by the most sensitive mechanical detectors. Dogs used in law enforcement have located marijuana smuggled by a truck loaded with onions.

The tracking dogs can locate hours-old tracks and then determine the direction of travel after following the tracks for only 5 to 6 feet; only one or two footprints! Tracking dogs have located their target subjects in deserts, following a track that was several days old and tracking over bedrock. Air scenting dogs routinely are employed to search bodies of water and have located targets submerged in 90 feet of salt water! In the mountains, it is not uncommon to have air scenting dogs alert to the presence of the subject on an adjacent ridge that may be miles away.

No trainer/handler can truly say that he/she knows how a dog uses his ability to "work" a scent. We can only make "educated guesses" based on our imperfect knowledge of "scent theory" and weather conditions. The best we can do is to guess where the scent <u>might</u> be located, and put our search dogs in the best position to follow the scent to its origin.

PRACTICAL SCENT THEORY

As a living organism metabolizes and decays, compounds are broken down and chemicals are created and released. In general terms seven distinct chemicals are present as a result of metabolism. Each of these chemicals possesses its own unique scent. These chemicals are exuded by the sweat glands and in the oils of the skin. When these seven chemicals, in varying concentrations, are present, their individual scents merge to form a unique scent made of the composite mix. The creation of scent happens in much the same way as a musical chord is made up of the combined tones of individual notes. The composite of the scents of the chemicals produced by the body is what gives each organism its unique scent. The combinations of the chemicals, and the varying concentrations that make up scent are influenced by diet, general health of the organism, and the mental state of the organism. To a dog, these combinations of chemicals form a "scent picture" which allows the dog to distinguish one organism's scent from another, even between members of the same species. In effect, what we humans may smell in black and white the dog smells in technicolor.

As dead skin cells slough (fall) from the body, they form "rafts", which are carried in the air, and deposited on the ground and on surrounding vegetation. They may also be washed from the body by rain, or water. These skin rafts carry the organism's scent. As the organism moves and disturbs the air around it, these rafts float in the resulting air currents and are scattered in the area the organism passes through leaving the organism's scent behind.

SCENT MOVEMENT

Nature tends to seek a balance and "works" to equalize differences in the concentration of molecules comprising a substance when it is introduced to a medium. For example, a fire introduces unburned particles of material (the molecules) into the air (the medium). We see those particles as "smoke". This tendency to equalize concentrations is called the Principal of Diffusion. Unless confined to an area by a barrier that the molecules cannot pass through,

Figure 7.6

the molecules will move from areas of higher concentration to areas of lower concentration.

Watching smoke rise from a fire and dissipate into the air, you see the smoke spreading out in various directions and dissipating into the air mass surrounding the fire. The smoke particles, individually, are too small to reflect enough light for your eye to detect. When the particles are leaving the fire, and are highly concentrated, they reflect enough light for your eye to detect and appear to form a "body", making the smoke visible. When the smoke particles are dispersed into the air and are less concentrated, the smoke seems to disappear into the air. **(See Figure 7.6)**

This is nature's effort to equalize the concentration of the smoke particles so that every unit volume of air surrounding the fire contains the same number of smoke particles. The particles are still there, but because they are no longer sufficiently concentrated to reflect enough light for your eye to see, they become "invisible". The particles then are carried by the air currents until deposited when the air cools and settles. Under calm conditions, the smoke particles remain concentrated and are carried as a body by the movement of the hot air as it rises. Eventually the particles will disperse themselves sufficiently to cool, and settle. In windier conditions the smoke particles are "scattered" as they leave the fire and the smoke dissipates more quickly.

Scent particles move in the air in much the same manner as the smoke particles. However, the Scent particles are much heavier than the smoke particles and they tend to fall from the air and be deposited more quickly.

for the dog to locate and follow. Unless the subject is still in the area emitting scent, the subject's scent will eventually diminish to the point that not even the best trained and most experienced search dog could locate. For the most part, search dogs are grouped into two categories: *Air Scenting and Tracking/Trailing*.

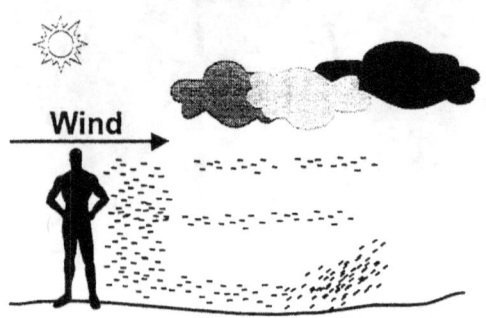

Figure 7.7

The scent rafts that are carried in the air currents are said to make up the **air scent**. These rafts float in the air currents and may be carried for several hundred meters before they are deposited. Like an object placed in moving water creates a wake on the downstream side, the air scent moves away from the organism and forms a three-dimensional "wake" of scent particles, called the **scent cone**, on the object's downwind side. **(See Figure 7.7)** Some rafts will be deposited in close proximity to the area the organism moved through and are said to make up the **trail scent**.

As the organism contacts the ground while moving through an area, the ground and vegetation are disturbed and the action of bacteria in the ground accelerates, itself creating a scent. This combination of broken vegetation, disturbed ground, and the accelerated action of the bacteria combine to form a composite scent. This is said to make up the **track scent. (See Figure 7.7)** As soon as the scent is deposited on objects and a track and trail are created, the scent begins to deteriorate or "age". With time the concentration of scent particles deteriorates to the point that very little scent will be present

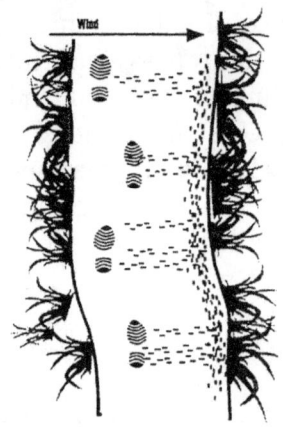

Figure 7.8

SEARCH AND RESCUE DOGS

AIR SCENTING DOGS

These dogs will seek out the subject's scent as it is carried in the air currents and he will "follow" the scent to its origin by moving in the direction where the scent is more concentrated. The dog will generally range (moving in wide sweeps), attempting to locate the "scent cone".

If the dog encounters the subject's trail, he may follow the trail scent when the air scent is not definitive enough to follow. The dog is trained and encouraged to "break" from the trail to follow the air scent when the air scent becomes stronger than the trail scent. These dogs generally work "off lead," that is without a leash.

TRACKING DOGS

The dog works the foot track (ground track) left by the subject by locating the scents left when the ground was disturbed by each

Chapter 7 - Search Techniques and Tactics

footprint. The "track scent" may be made up of broken vegetation, the increased activity of bacteria when the sand/dirt is disturbed, the transfer of material from one area to another, and even the scent left by the sole of the subject's shoe. These dogs generally work "on lead"; that is, with a leash to their handler. **(See Figure 7.8)**

TRAILING DOG

As the subject passes through an area, skin rafts are deposited along the route of the track and this creates a "trail" of scent. The dog will "cast" (moving side to side) as he "associates" the scent of the individual creating the track to the track itself. The Tracking/Trailing Dog will work on the down wind side of the track, from the track to the trail, preferring to locate the scent that is strongest at that particular moment. These dogs generally work "on lead".

Generally, only dogs that participate in tracking competitions truly track exclusively. What has been thought of as a "Tracking Dog" is actually a Tracking/Trailing Dog. Over the years numerous "sub-specialties" for search dogs have emerged, among these are:

AVALANCHE DOGS

Because the subject's body temperature is higher than the temperature of the snow that he/she is buried in, any air that may be trapped around the body will rise to the surface of the snow and carry the subject's scent with it. The dog will "alert" (signal his handler), and indicate the presence of the scent by barking and digging at the surface of the snow over the subject's position. Both airscenting or tracking/trailing dogs have been successfully trained in avalanche work.

CADAVER DOGS

Both air scenting and tracking/trailing dogs have been specially trained in locating deceased persons in a variety of locations. Normally, search dogs are trained to locate living subjects and will locate the deceased by virtue of a behavior different from finding a live person.

DISASTER DOGS

These are dogs that will search in, around and under collapsed structures to locate and indicate (by barking and digging) the presence of humans. Both air scenting and tracking/trailing dogs are employed in this specialty.

WATER SEARCH DOGS

This skill is held by air scenting dogs that have been trained to locate the subject's scent rising from the surface of a body of water. These air scent dogs generally work from a boat with their handler who interprets what the dog is 'saying' to the boat operator who maneuvers the boat over the place where the scent is the strongest.

For the purposes of this text we will confine our discussion to air scenting and tracking/trailing dogs.

SCENT DOG TRAINING

Most Search Dog Crews spend untold hours training and preparing their search dogs (and themselves) to become mission ready. Training and working with a scenting dog is a complex art. To become proficient requires a considerable amount of time, energy and effort.

- The handler/trainer must be knowledgeable in scent theory and scent makeup. He/she should know about weather and the movement of air currents (not only day-to-day weather changes, but the movement of air minute-to-minute).
- The handler/trainer should have an exceptional grasp of dog training procedures and philosophies so that he/she can train the dog.
- A puppy must be selected based on specific criteria. The puppy will need to be "socialized" (a continual introduction to new people, places and areas). The handler/trainer must ensure that each introduction results in a positive experience for the dog, be-

cause later it will be difficult to ask the dog to find something that he has decided he doesn't like. The prospective Search dog will need to be trained in obedience, agility *and* doing the scent work.

- The handler/trainer will create exercises for the dog that will stimulate him and will attempt to simulate challenges that the dog/handler crew *may* expect to encounter in the field. Every training session is designed with the success of the dog in mind. The axiom of the search dog handler/trainer is that the search dog *ALWAYS* succeeds!

TRAINING THE AIR SCENT DOG

Traditionally, Air Scenting Dogs are trained to find a subject by using the airborne scent that the handler/trainer has hidden in varying places. The handler/trainer knows that the "subject" is in the area being searched and it becomes a matter of time before the air scent dog-in-training locates the "subject". Generally, neither the dog being trained, nor the handler/trainer is concerned with signs left by the subject. In fact, the handler/trainer may even discourage the dog from tracking/trailing the subject by bringing the dog into the training area from a direction different than the one used by the subject.

The dog is encouraged to continue a search of the area until the subject is located by the air scent alone. This is thought to encourage the air scenting dog to locate the subject quickly and continue working until he/she succeeds, and the dog receives a reward for achieving the goal.

As the air scent dog progresses in his/her training, the dog is brought to the training ground and trained to alert the handler to the presence of the air scent. When the dog's alert is evident, the dog may then be further encouraged by the handler to locate the subject. As training progresses the dog is trained to return to the handler/trainer, indicating that the subject has been located. The dog is then given a command to "re-find" the subject with the handler following. Remember that the air scent dog works "off lead" and may be at a distance and out of sight of the handler when he/she locates the air scent. The "re-find" assures that the dog will lead the handler to the subject.

Few handler/trainers actually train their air scent dogs to search areas that they, the handler/trainers, know contain clues but no subject to find. In the actual search mission, obviously, there can be no guarantee that the subject will be in the area that the air scent dog will be assigned to search, but the subject may well have passed through. Without evidence that the subject is indeed in the area being searched, it would be unreasonable to expect an air scenting dog to attempt to locate "something to find" when he/she may never have been faced with such a task.

TRAINING THE TRACKING/TRAILING DOG

Tracking/trailing dogs are trained to follow a track that has been laid by the subject until he/she reaches the end of the track and the dog receives his reward. Tracking/trailing dogs work on lead, with their handlers following, and therefore, there is generally no need to train them to "re-find" the subject. The speed at which the tracking/trailing dog works the track is dependent on the age of the track, the dog itself, (some breeds tend to be more meticulous than other breeds and tend to work more slowly), and, of course, the ability of the handler to keep up with the dog.

SCENT DISCRIMINATION

Both tracking/trailing and air scenting dogs can be trained to "discriminate" scent. That is, to locate *only* the subject that has created the scent they have been asked to follow. This training involves obtaining an article that has been handled (or worn) by the subject which is then "shown" to the dog. The dog then locates the track or scent cone that matches the scent on the article he/she has been shown, and the dog proceeds to locate the subject. With the high number of searchers that may be in the search area, scent discrimination helps the dog handler locate only the subject of the search and not other searchers.

Because there may be many foot-tracks in the search area, some of which will have been left by the searchers and only one left by the subject, most all tracking/trailing dogs are trained in scent discrimination. Without scent discrimination training, it would be a huge waste of time, and of the resource, to follow a track to its conclusion only to locate another search crew! These dogs are generally more clue conscious and may also indicate objects that may have been dropped by the subject along the track as he/she passes through the area.

Some air scent dogs are trained in scent discrimination. However, most will locate any human in their search area. In some instances, the air scent dog may alert the handler to the presence of humans in adjacent areas. When the air scenting dog shows a high degree of interest (alerts) in an area, the direction of the alert is usually reported to the control point (Incident Command). Incident Command can then advise the handler of the presence (or absence) of other search crews in the dog's area of interest and the handler can either follow up on the alert or discard the alert and "restart" the dog working.

It should be noted that scent dogs are not training specific, i.e., tracking/trailing trained dogs will still air scent and air scent trained dogs will track and trail. Nor is it essential that a scent article be available to show to the scent discrimination trained dog. Any well trained scenting dog will gladly work for the handler and will adapt as the situation warrants. As a rule though, the scenting dog will be better practiced in one of these disciplines.

Scent dog training may leave the handler/trainer little, if any, time to learn and practice sign cutting and clue consciousness skills leaving quite a number of handlers preferring to rely on the dog to show them any important signs of the subject. Unfortunately, some search dogs work so fast that they may "blow by" and ignore significant signs in their effort to locate a strong scent.

A SEARCH DOG CREW/ SEARCH CREW TASK FORCE

Presently, there is a movement among some dog search units to begin teaching and practicing sign cutting and clue consciousness skills, as well as the balance of the SAR Tech™ skills. In Europe these skills are learned and practiced by dog handlers before they ever begin to train a dog in an effort to create an effective and efficient search dog crew (crew = handler + dog). Until this becomes common practice in your area, the SAR TECH™ I/Crewleader III™ will be required to incorporate the dog crew into your search crew when searching your assigned areas. As a part of the pre-planning for future search missions, contact the dog search units in your area and ask for their unit's standards of training and evaluation for the handlers and dogs. Investigate and get to know the potential resource prior to calling them, and their incorporation into the search effort will be much smoother.

When looking at the dog unit's "Standards of Training and Evaluation", pay particular attention to how that unit trains and evaluates the dog and handler for alerts, re-finds, obedience and aggression (both towards other dogs and towards people). The object of the search mission is to get the search crew to the subject. The issue is whether this unit's dog/handler crews can materially assist the search manager to accomplish that aspect of the mission.

Sadly and all too often, the SAR dog crews are called in when the search for a subject has "gone to the dogs". Hundreds of ground based personnel ("ground pounders") (police officers, fire fighters, National Guard, and well-intentioned volunteers, *including* SAR TECH™ trained people) have scoured the areas and come up "empty handed". Frustrated search managers, and a myriad of scents usually await the search dog handler when the search is "dumped in his lap" for resolution. "Let us know what you find" is generally the last thing the handler hears as the Incident Commander drives away.

Most handlers would appreciate having a definite LKP and an indication of the subject's direction of travel to start their dogs working. Virtually every search dog handler, either air scenting or tracking/trailing, dreams of having the opportunity to join in a search effort, being told that there is conclusive evidence of the subject in a specific area (a high POA), and then being asked to locate the subject.

If we maintain the philosophy that "Search is an Emergency", and if we truly are expected to "Manage the Search Function," then we should make the maximum use of our available resources in a manner that will assure the greatest chance for success of the overall mission.

The Search Manager will determine the "target" *cumulative* POD for the overall search area, and the crewleaders will be tasked with accomplishing the highest possible POD's for their crews. If the Manager's target is a 95% efficiency, then the reported POD's for each crew's pass through the area will be added together until the target efficiency is met. Only when the cumulative POD is accomplished will the decision to either expand the search area, or, suspend the mission be made.

When we contemplate the efficiency of single resources (the smallest number that can accomplish a function) into a single effort (task force), we must allow for basic differences in the resources that will be incorporated.

Search dogs and search technicians are trained and practiced in two *differing* methods of conducting a Search mission.

The SAR TECH™ has been trained to locate as many clues and signs (evidence) of the subject's passing over varying terrain as possible, and to follow this trail of evidence to the subject. During testing, when the evidence is evaluated for purposes of search efficiency, they must meet a 50% POD (based on the number of clues found), on each part of the search station, area search and route search using a CS=1. During actual searches, well trained and experienced SAR TECH™ crews, using established search techniques, can document a POD approaching 50%, under ideal conditions.

As a result of their training methods, (the search dog is trained to locate the subject, using only one piece of evidence —the subject's scent.), search dogs become "subject oriented". This tends to give the scenting dog a low POD. Furthermore, there really is no method for determining the POD for a dog. If they find the subject, or his scent; their POD is considered 100%. If they don't, their POD is assumed to be 0. Because tracking/trailing dogs are generally started from the LKP, on the subject's track, their POD is considered higher than the air scenting dog who is asked to locate first the scent, and then the subject, over the entire search segment. The tracking/trailing dog is "given" a 100% POD when he "takes" the track. In some places the air scenting dog is assigned a POD of 45% for the purposes of statistics.

The objective is to make the maximum use of the available resources, to search the area efficiently and spend the least amount of "searcher hours". This would suggest that the best combination of the resources is one that incorporates the highest and best use of each skill. With the proper use of the dog resource, the efficiency rating of the task force can become significant. Factoring the efficiency of the SAR TECH™ Crew that has a potential 50% POD, *plus* the tracking/trailing dog would give the task force a potential (POD Accumulated) of 73% when starting from the LKP. The SAR TECH™ crew with an air scenting dog would nearly accomplish the target cumulative POD for an area in one pass!

The Search Task Force Leader must make decisions based on the crew's assigned task and the type of resource assigned; tracking/trailing or air scenting. This assignment may be a Hasty, or Efficient Search of the assigned area to locate evidence (sign) and "chase the subject down" by tracking/trailing, or position his crew in the subject's direction of travel and "cut the subject off" by air scenting.

In either case, it will make little difference to search crews that rely on sight alone from which direction an area is searched. To the dog, the direction he/she approaches the search area may be of critical importance. All search dogs work best when working into the wind. When the area is approached with the scenting dog in mind (particularly the air scenting dog) the crew can work in wider sweeps, covering more area with each pass and cover the area more quickly and more reliable.

AIR MOVEMENT

Air tends to move from cooler areas where the air is more dense (and heavier) to warmer areas where the air is less dense (and lighter) obeying the same rules of diffusion that governs the movement of particles in the air. The sun as the source of heat, drives the mechanism of air movement. As the sun warms the ground, heat radiates from the ground and the air covering the ground is warmed. This warmed air then rises and cooler air that has not been over the ground the sun has warmed moves in to fill the "space" (void) left when the warmer air rises. **(See Figure 7.9)**

Inconsistencies of the earth's surface create differing warming and cooling rates of the air masses that cover the surface. Variations in the warming and cooling of the air masses creates the movements of the air as a mass and winds are born. The amount of heating or cooling determines the amount of air movement that is driven by the temperature differential. The greater the differences in temperature (cool to warm) the more forceful the movement of the air, and the wider the area that will be affected by that movement. Though the movement of air may not be perceptible to you, the air is moving even in the calmest of conditions.

The many variations of the earth's surface effects the warming and cooling rates of the air mass. There are certainly conditions present that affect air movement on a global scale and have effect on our local areas. For the most part we are only concerned with the movement of air in our search area and specifically in our search segment, perhaps only in the immediate area we are working now.

The different warming and cooling rates of one area relative to another, effects the direction of the air movement. You need to remember this: air will generally be drawn from a cool area to a warming area.

TOPOGRAPHY OF THE TERRAIN

When the terrain is more varied, more shadows are produced and the air over the terrain is warmed unevenly. As the sun rises in the mountains, the ridges are first to be lit by the sun's rays and are warmed before the valleys. The air over the ridges rises and the air from the valleys moves up to fill in the void. This movement creates "thermals" that rise up the slope carrying the scents up from the valley. As the sun sets, the valleys cool quickly and the air settles rapidly, drawing the air from the ridges and the air movement reverses, now carrying the scents from the ridges down into the valleys.

VEGETATION COVERING THE TOPOGRAPHY

The vegetation is a different color (usually darker) than that of the ground (usually lighter), and darker colors generally warm faster than lighter colors. In the morning, as the sun rises and the vegetation warms before the open field, the cooler air covering the field will move toward the vegetated area filling the void. This condition will last for only a short time. Later in the day, the field (which is sun lit) will be warmer than the vegetated area (which is

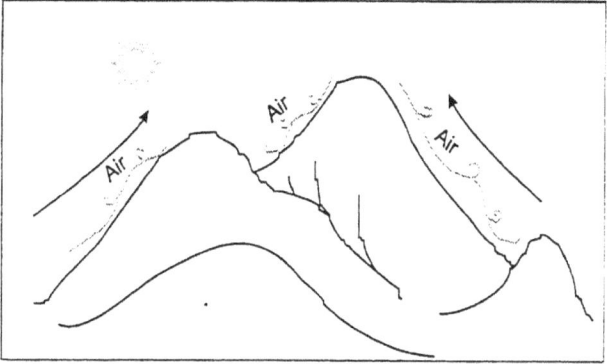

Figure 7.9

shaded), and the air will move from the shaded area to the sun lit field. A stand of trees in a field presents a large surface area to the sun and the trees (and surrounding air) are warmed as the sun rises. When the cooler air moves toward the trees the scents present in the field are carried toward the trees. Experienced air scent dog handlers have learned that their dogs can "clear" an entire field by working the area around a stand of trees in the field in the early morning.

THE DENSITY OF THE VEGETATION

When the vegetation is dense (particularly forested as opposed to grass covered), the top of the vegetation presents a surface that is warmed by the sun. The warm air over the vegetation rises. The coloring is darker and warms faster relative to the surrounding bare ground, but a new variation is added by the shadowing effect of the vegetation which cools the ground below it. Open areas, that receive sunlight, within the forested areas, that are shaded, add yet another variation. The cool air from the shadowed areas attempts to replace the rising air above the vegetation but is blocked by the leaves. The air will tend to move to the open areas (sun lit or not) and will be drawn upward. Air will move from the shaded areas carrying the scents from the shade to the open areas. This is called the "chimney effect". If the open area is sun lit, this chimney effect will be enhanced and the air will be drawn even faster from the shaded areas carrying the scents from farther away.

BODIES OF WATER

Almost universally, as the sun shines on an area containing a body of water, the ground adjacent to the water will be warmer than the body of water. The warm air over the land will rise and the air over the water will move "ashore" to fill the void carrying the scents from the water to the land. At night, the land will give up its heat faster than the water will, and the air movement will reverse, moving from the land to the water, carrying the scents toward the water. A "sea" breeze during the day and a "land" breeze at night.

As the air "flows" over the terrain, it forms currents. Knowledge of the currents further allows the Handler to work with his partner to locate the source of the scents carried by the air. Using this knowledge of air movement is what allows the handler to use the terrain to move the scenting dog into the areas that will enhance the chances for success.

Using the topography of the terrain principle above, the best place for the air scenting dog to work a mountainous area during the day is along the ridges. This will put him in a position where the scents of the subject presumed to be in the valley below are being brought to his nose. Conversely, the best place to employ the air scenting dog at night, to cover the same area, would be in the valley.

Using the vegetation covering the topography principle, it is best to work the dog along the border between a field and the forest. The scents from the field would be brought to him in the early morning and the scents from the wooded area would be brought to him later in the day. You and the handler would have to know from which area the scents (if any) would be coming. Also, the handler might be able to use the dog to search an entire field by working the area around a stand of trees, during the right time of day.

Using the density of the vegetation principle, the handler might seek out an open area within a forested area to take advantage of the chimney effect when working a forested area.

Bodies of water that may be encountered within the search area might be covered by working the dog along the shore line. Conversely, using the body of water, the area adjacent to the water can be covered also by working the shore line at night.

The direction of the air movement is also important to the tracking/trailing dog. Even though this scenting dog relies less on the airborne scent than does an air scent dog, wind direction will still have an effect on his ability to work.

Now, based on your knowledge of air movement, when employing a scenting dog in your crew, your decision making process involves us-

Chapter 7 - Search Techniques and Tactics

ing the topographic map to determine the best position to insert your crew and from what direction you will be best able to accomplish your assigned mission.

Figure 7.7 is a suggested algorithm entitled "Lost Subject Flowchart". Obviously, the objective of any search is to begin at a Point Last Seen (PLS) and attempt to locate a Last Known Point (LKP), if it is different than the PLS. And, to locate the subject.

PLEASE LOOK AT THE LEFT SIDE OF THE CHART

LOST SUBJECT FLOWCHART

Figure 7.10

(See Figure 7.10)

Once the PLS has been located, the area should be investigated using a crew configured with both SAR TECH™ and scenting dogs. If the dog is able to "work the scent", the SAR TECH™ will become support for the dog/handler crew. If the dog won't work the scent, the SAR TECH™ should follow the evidence, tracking the subject visually until the conditions become more favorable for the dog.

When the conditions improve, retry the dog on the scent.

- Areas where articles are located, or ar-

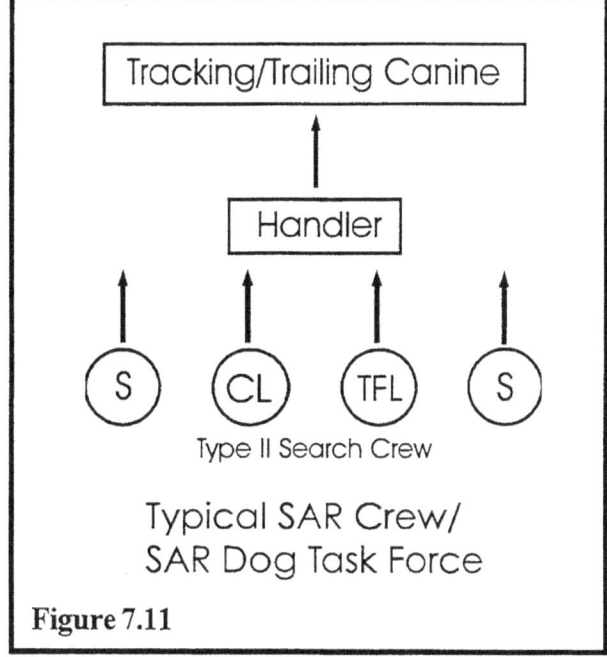

Figure 7.11

eas where the subject may have stopped for a time, may be the best place to "retry" the dog. In summary, any time the location of the LKP is updated, retry the dog.
- The crew should pay particular attention to weather changes (wind, temperature, sun light, rain and humidity) and the time of day because changes to the positive in any of these variables may also indicate times in which to retry the dog.
- If possible, the crewleader should keep the crew on the downwind side of the assigned area to give the dog better advantage to pick up airborne scent.

At the point that the dog is able to work the scent, the SAR TECH™ should become support for the dog/handler crew, assisting in land navigation, orienteering and communications. The sign-cutters should remain aware of the evidence (track) encountered while the dog is working, and the Search Crewleader should be prepared to resume (or assume) tracking in the event the dog "loses" the scent. One configuration for the combined crew is to have the dog in front, followed by the handler. The visual tracking crew follows the dog and handler with the "point" behind the handler (allowing some distance) and the flankers follow in their usual position. **(See Figure 7.11)**

In this configuration, should the direction of the foot track of the subject change abruptly and the dog miss the change, the visual trackers will notice the new direction of the track. The dog and Handler, generally, will be following the scent trail on the downwind side of the track, and they should not interfere with the actual foot track itself. With some coordination, it should present little problem to change roles during the mission.

PLEASE LOOK AT THE RIGHT SIDE OF THE CHART (See Figure 7.10)

In the absence of a PLS (or LKP), the crews, made up of SAR TECH™ and scent dogs conduct Class I searches for evidence and scent. The trails might be "swept" to create track traps and to confine the subject to an area. Any strong alerts, and the direction of the alerts, by the dog should be noted, reported to command and reported again during debriefing.

The crews should report to command any areas that may appear to be natural attractions. The commander will want to have those areas searched. Used appropriately, the dog can "check out" most areas in much less time than would be required of SAR crew working by sight alone.

Further, the crews should note areas they believe maybe best searched by a dog and report these to command during debriefing so that these areas may be considered when the search moves beyond Class I to Class II searches.

At any point that an LKP is identified, the flow chart will move to the left and the balance of the algorithm followed from LKP.

FURTHER CONSIDERATIONS

1. Use of dogs should not supplant other resources. There is no reason that any other resource should be withheld from the search mission in favor of air scenting or tracking/trailing dogs.
2. Dog crews should be able to work in and around operations involving other search crews, including other dog crews. Search dogs should enjoy their work. <u>Any signs of aggression</u>, either toward other dogs, and particularly, toward people, <u>should never be tolerated for any reason!</u>
3. Dog unit leaders should be actively involved in the Planning Section of the Incident Command Post for consultation on the best use of the dog resource. They are very familiar with their dog partners and as such, can give you valuable and time saving insight on how best to employ the resource.
4. In some areas, during certain times of the year, and under certain weather conditions, the track scent may only last for several hours. The air scent will deteriorate at an even faster rate. It has been determined that at 85 degrees with 85% humidity, the critical spacing for air scenting dogs may be as close as 8 meters.

Handlers of tracking/trailing dogs generally prefer moist, vegetated areas with a calm or barely palpable breeze to give their partners the best conditions in which to work. Handlers of air scenting dogs prefer conditions that are either warming, cooling or drying and a gentle breeze, to giver their partners the best conditions to work in. During and after a gentle rain, with the ground drying, is an excellent time to employ both types of scenting dog. Generally speaking; hotter, drier, windier conditions will present the most difficulty for any scenting dog.

The most effective time to employ a scenting dog is early, and late in the day. Similar to the best time to man-track. Most handlers believe that the longer their shadow the better

Chapter 7 - Search Techniques and Tactics   113

the time of day.

For dogs who are agile and have agile handlers, nighttime is an excellent time to work. Handlers of air scenting dogs that routinely work "off lead", must assure that their dogs have reliable "re-finds", as the handlers will find it very difficult to watch their dogs in the dark.

DO'S AND DONT'S
1. When evidence of the subject's passing (track) has been located and a scenting dog is employed, make every attempt to secure the area and keep people out. This will allow the dog the best opportunity to work the area and pick up the scents associated with the subject. If man-trackers follow the track, they will be adding their scent to the subject's trail of scent and the dog may find the composite confusing. Flag or "rope off" the area with tape, if you must mark the track, use your stick as opposed to your foot.
2. Do not handle articles the subject may have dropped. The dog handler can touch and pick up the article to "show" it to the dog. If someone other than the handler touches the article, their scent will be added to the subject's scent. It you are securing a scent article for a scent discriminating dog, handle the article with tongs and (if possible) place the article in a paper bag. Plastic is made of hydrocarbons and the plastic bag itself will add that scent to the article, and may confuse the dog.
3. Provide an airy, well ventilated location for the scenting dogs to stage while in base camp. Gasoline, motor oils and vehicle exhaust are the worst contamination possible for the scent dog. One whiff of gasoline vapor may destroy a scenting dog's ability to detect scent for up to 4 hours.
4. Call the scent dogs in early in the search effort. As with SAR TECH™, dogs utilize their own experiences to solve new and different challenges. Older, more experienced scenting dogs develop a "cold nose" and will be able to detect older scents that younger, less experienced dogs will miss. As time decays the scents, fewer scent dogs will be able to work in the search effort and the overall effectiveness of the dog will diminish. From your own experience you know that the sooner you can get started in resolving the search, the better the evidence that will be available to give you the best chances for success.

Chapter 7 - Search Techniques and Tactics

REVIEW QUESTIONS

1. Define Probability of Detection. _____
   _____

2. List three factors that might affect the Search Crew's Probability of Detection.
   _____

3. Define scanning. _____
   _____

4. Define observing. _____

5. Searching for signs left by a subject passing through an area is referred to as?
   _____

6. List three factors that will improve clue awareness.
   _____   _____

7. Dividing search segments into smaller segments and then searching the perimeters of the smaller segments to determine if the subject has moved from one segment to another is referred to as?
   _____

8. List some Passive Search Tactics:
   _____   _____

9. List some Active Search Tactics:
   _____   _____

10. A small, fast moving, highly trained search crew looking for the lost subject(s) or clue(s) is what level or class of search tactic?
    _____

11. A slower, more methodical search of an area with unskilled or semi-skilled search crews working at less that critical spacing is an example of a:
    _____

12. Define Critical Spacing.
    _____
    _____
    _____

Chapter 7 - Search Techniques and Tactics   ■ 115

13. The method for determining critical spacing is called?
    _____

14. List some terrain features that would be useful for determining a route search:
    _____ _____
    _____ _____

15. Describe the differences between air scenting dogs and tracking/trailing dogs.
    _____
    _____
    _____

16. Define the following when applied to scenting canines:

Casting: _____

Ranging: _____

17. Training the scenting canine to locate only the subject "belonging" to the scent article is a definition of:
    _____

18. In general, air moves from _____ areas toward _____ areas.

19. In general, in the mountains, air moves up-slope during the _____

and down-slope during the _____ .

20. Describe a method for securing an article which has been dropped by the subject for use as a scent article.
    _____
    _____

NOTES:

Chapter 8 - Briefing & Debriefing

BRIEFING & DEBRIEFING

OBJECTIVES

A. The student shall explain the information necessary and exchanged during a briefing.

B. The student will be able to list and explain the information that must be obtained during a mission briefing.

C. The student will be able to explain the five (5) parts of a crew operations assignment briefing.

D. The student shall, given the proper briefing information, demonstrate briefing his/her crew members on an operational assignment.

E. The student shall explain the need for crew debriefing as it relates to the management of a SAR incident.

F. The student shall list the information needed to be prepared for a debriefing.

BRIEFING

People are most effective when they are well informed about all aspects of the situation at a search incident. And, people who feel they are not important enough to be given details about the operation are more likely to be less enthusiastic about a search especially after they have been under stress and are suffering from fatigue. Morale is important.

In addition to complete oral briefings, a written briefing serves as future reference for all personnel. The written briefing can be as detailed as necessary to provide complete and up-to-date information about the situation, past, present, and future.

The type and purpose of the briefing dictates the kind and amount of information that is included in the briefing.

DEFINITIONS

GENERAL BRIEFING

A summary of the situation, past and present, that provides information that will help orient everyone on the search team to all facets of the incident.

OPERATIONAL BRIEFING (Crew Briefing)

Operational briefings offer authoritative information and instructions to Search Crews, Task Forces, and Strike Teams having primary involvement and assignment of a missions during a search. During the operational briefing is when crews and teams are given their mission assignments.

In this portion of the text, we will concentrate on the Operational Briefing. Searchers need guidance and accurate information if they are to get the job done, efficiently and with the best possible results. Without this guidance people cannot be expected to know what clues to search for, who are they searching for, or what area they are to search.

A briefing should also include direction about the techniques a crew is expected to employ and an indication of how carefully they are to search their assigned areas. The expectations of POD for the mission should be an important part of a crew's assignment and crew briefing.

The Crewleader normally should receive the operational briefing from the operations section manager and then he/she, in turn, briefs his/her crew, task force or strike team about the mission. The crew members should be encouraged to ask questions about the assignment. If the Crewleader needs additional information to answer his/her crew's questions, the answers should be obtained and distributed before leaving camp to begin the assignment. The Crewleader should then "brief back" the mission to the operations section manager so that it is clear to everyone that the mission is understood by all and it will be properly executed. To execute the wrong mission is a waste of time and may be life-threatening for the victim.

The following information needs to be known before beginning an assignment.

1. The crew should know how clues should be handled. Specific procedures or requirements for clue marking and/or retrieval must be defined in advance. Incorrect handling of evidence or waiting in the field for instructions can waste a lot of precious time or ruin the value of important clues.

2. The Crewleader must know what type of field assistance he/she can count on. If a victim is found and is in need of medical attention and transport, the crewleader must know what type of help and back up is available. In many situations it is just as likely that a member of the search team could be injured and need medical assistance and transport. The Crewleader must know exactly what resources are available to his/her own crew members, and he/she needs to know how to access that help.

3. If the search crew needs special equipment to either accomplish a mission or to facilitate the crew's comfort or

Chapter 8 - Briefing & Debriefing

safety, the crewleader needs to address these needs in a briefing. What safety considerations and hazards might a crew face? Safety needs must be anticipated.

4. Many times searchers need to be aware of certain external influences and how to handle them as required by the Incident Commander.
5. Once the crew has returned from a mission the record of their activities will need to be prepared and presented to the Incident Commander. It is important to know what type of debriefing the Incident Commander expects to receive. If you don't know in advance what is expected you probably will not collect the type of information he/she is looking for. You also need to know how detailed your debriefing must be.

To insure that no important information is omitted from the information given to the crew or strike team, some uniform format is needed.

Rather than experiment with forms and formats, we recommend you use the standard format used by the American military. The standard five part military operation order is well suited for this type of SAR briefing. This briefing style works hand in glove with the ICS type of information transfer used during a search. The reason the military order works so well with ICS is ICS, itself, is an adaptation of military command.

All the information required by a crew or strike team can be arranged in this operation order. Once individuals are familiar with the parts of the operation order, it becomes easy for the crew members to organize their thinking according to the standard format and to follow the briefing format to prepare themselves for an assignment. The 5 parts of the uniform operations order are:

1) **Situation** - What has happened, what is happening and what is expected to happen.
2) **Mission** (Task assignment) - *What* the unit is assigned to do.
3) **Execution** - Detail plan of *how* the unit will accomplish the assignment.
4) **Administration and Logistics** - Equipment and support.
5) **Communications and Command** - Procedures and information.

Each of these parts can be broken down into subsections with each subsection containing detailed information about the assignment of the resource (team) and its members.

CREW OR STRIKE TEAM OPERATIONS ORDER

SITUATION - (as it affects the resource)

- Subject Information - what we know about the person we are looking for.
- Complete physical description of the person.
- Clothing worn and equipment carried by the person.
- Physical and mental condition of the person.
- Behavioral traits of the person.
- Circumstances surrounding the search. How it came about that this person was missing.
- Medical/health problems of the person.
- Photo if one is available.
- Clue consideration.
- Sole pattern of footwear.
- Items he/she is believed to be carrying.
- Subject's trip plans.
- Missions and locations of search resources on the right or left as well as information on search resources in the search area prior to this mission.
- Attachments working with the search resource:
  - Dogs
  - Aircraft
  - Specialists
- Weather conditions forecast at present and anticipated during the mission.

MISSION

Describes the unit's specific objective; that is, what this unit is to accomplish, and the segment in which it is to be done. **Referenced from the ICS Form 204.**

EXECUTION

Describes the overall plan to be used during the operation. Explains the overall assignments of individuals, crews and/or strike teams and specific duties during the search mission. Provides details of the tactical assignment with explicit instructions about where and how to search. Such as:

- Specific area to search.
- Configuration, spacing of the searchers.
- Where to start and stop.
- Where the adjacent units will be.
- Who will be responsible for:
  - navigation,
  - tally,
  - documentation, and
  - other specialized tasks.
- Coordinating instructions. (Applying to all personnel)
- Times of departure and return.
- Transportation details.
- Routes and navigation.
- General Information.
- Organization of personnel.
- Expected POD.
- Method of handling, marking, and reporting clues.
- How to handle external influences such as family and media.
  - Markings used to identify them.
  - Where to refer them for authoritative information.
- Instructions for subject contact:
  - Dead
  - Injured
  - Well
- Rescue/evacuation plan.
- Scene protection.
- Safety instructions.
- Specific things to watch for.
- What to do if...
- Reporting details, what, when, and how?
- What to do if member of unit is injured.
- Debriefing procedures
  - Where and when, and with whom.
  - What information to be required and what format and what level of detail will be required.
- Place and time for pre-departure inspection.

ADMINISTRATION AND LOGISTICS

- Food & water.
- Special equipment.
  - What specific equipment.
  - Carried by whom.
  - Where to obtain.
- Location of medical assistance.
  - How to contact.
  - Estimated time it will take to get to the scene.

COMMUNICATIONS AND COMMAND

- Communications equipment.
  - Radio frequency(s) to be used.
  - Call signs.
  - Codes.
  - Other type signals.
    - Hand and arm.
    - Light.
    - Sound.
- Regular reporting times.
- Command.
  - Chain of command within unit(s).
  - Location of leader during various phases of this mission.

The crew briefing should be given far enough in advance to allow members of the crew/strike team to prepare themselves and their equipment and obtain and prepare any special equipment needed for their assignments.

The briefing should be given in an area that is free from distractions, sheltered from the elements, and large enough to comfortably accommodate the unit being briefed.

All visual aids, such as maps, terrain models, blackboards, aerial photos should be used to make sure each member understands the mission. If visual aids are not available, planned actions are sketched on the ground.

In order to minimize interruptions during the briefing everyone is expected to take notes and to ask his/her questions when the leader completes his/her explanation. And when the explanation has been completed it is important that the leader provide enough time to give thorough answers to the questions raised by the crew members.

When all members of the crew or strike team fully understand the assignment and what responsibilities they, as individual members, have towards the assignment, the success of the mission is greatly increased. Therefore it is very important for the leadership to take the time to make sure everybody understands what he/she is supposed to do and to also understand where he/she fits into the mission. Don't assume a person understands just because he/she has not asked questions.

An accurate, thorough, and efficient briefing will greatly influence the outcome of the mission, the crew's ability to actually accomplish the mission, and the ultimate outcome of the search.

DEBRIEFING

In order for the management team to make the most effective use of information gathered by field personnel during a mission, the field personnel must be given an opportunity to meet with management to tell them exactly what they were able to accomplish, what they saw, and what opinions they created.

Debriefing is a complete interview of a field search unit to gain a thorough understanding of all evidence and activities encountered during the mission. Always remember that the crew members themselves may not understand the full importance of what they are reporting. Therefore encourage them to share all their observations. The more experienced management team may be able to draw conclusions which are not evident to the individual team members.

Debriefing is usually conducted by the Situation Unit of the Planning Section and done according to ICS guidelines. On larger incidents it may be that the leader of a Crew/Task Force/Strike Team is the only person from each team who is debriefed. However, when possible, the entire crew should attend the debriefing. Each person's observations are important.

THE PURPOSE OF DEBRIEFING

The debriefing process gathers, through a complete interview of the searchers, all the information necessary to develop a complete, accurate understanding of that team's prior field activities and clue evidence. It is the information management needs to plan the next search strategies and tactics.

Without thorough and accurate information, subsequent planning may be unrealistic, misdirected or incomplete. The crewleader needs to document as much detailed information as possible so that the following questions can be adequately answered. Without having good answers to the following questions future missions could be ineffective. **(See NASAR Debriefing Form)**

- Without exaggerations, what exactly did the team members actually accomplish?
- What is the estimated probability of detection (POD)?
- What were the locations of any clues, regardless of how insignificant they may seem to the searcher?
- Were there any gaps in coverage or search difficulties encountered? It is critical to know what wasn't searched.
- Are there any hazards in the area?
- Were there any problems encountered with the communications?
- Are there any suggestions, ideas or recommendations from the searchers to consider during future missions?

It is very important that all information be as precise as possible concerning:
- Areas covered.
- Any gap that occurred.
- Estimated POD of the search.

Incomplete or inaccurate information in these areas will certainly cause inaccurate planning data for future efforts. Therefore it is the responsibility of the debriefer to ask the right questions and to probe for meaningful answers. Remember that the individual searcher knows only what he/she has experienced and does not have the context of all the information that is coming in from many other searchers. The debriefer is in a position to put the clues together. Therefore it is up to the debriefer to collect the facts by asking questions.

Debriefers may to have to resort to actually "picking the brains" of the members being debriefed in order to ensure getting as much information as possible from them. The success of the entire mission may depend on some little fact that may seem totally irrelevant.

As many crew members as possible should attend the briefing to ensure that everyone feels that their input is important and to gather as many points of observation as possible. As much debriefing as possible should be done on an individual basis and as soon as possible after the resource returns from the field.

In order to insure accuracy and proper documentation debriefings should be written. Try to confirm information by getting it from more than one source.

Searchers should bring to the debriefing their maps, sketches, photos, and a 214 form with notes. Use of these documents help to ensure the information gathered is objective, complete and accurate. It will also tend to jog memories so that the debriefings will contain information as complete as possible.

Don't try to depend on memory. As the search operation progresses and the number of missions accumulate, people tend to forget what happened and when it happened. Debriefing information should be written on a debriefing form to ensure the accurate recording of this information. The debriefing form **(See NASAR Debriefing Form)** should be attached to the Crew/Task Force/Strike Team 204 form and 214 form to be added to the information gathered by the Situation Unit of the Planning Section. It is very valuable to reread past debriefing reports. They give a very accurate picture of how the search is progressing.

In summary, debriefing is an effective tool for evaluating present successes and for forming a foundation of facts on which to build future mission plans.

Effective debriefing:
- Is thorough. It leaves no stone unturned.
- Is timely.
- Focuses on individual belief as well as the objective facts.
- Is written.
- Includes recommendations of the searchers and search leaders.

Chapter 8 - Briefing & Debriefing

DEBRIEFING FORM	1. INCIDENT NAME	2. DATE PREPARED	3. TIME PREPARED
4. OPERATIONAL PERIOD	5. DATE OF ASSIGNMENT	6. BEGIN ASSIGNMENT	7. END ASSIGNMENT
8. DEBRIEFER	9. MEMBERS AT BRIEFING		
EXPLAIN WHAT YOU DID DURING YOUR ASSIGNMENT			
ESTIMATE POD'S FOR ASSIGNMENT			
DESCRIBE ANY CLUES AND THEIR LOCATION (UTM) AND THE CURRENT STATUS OF THE CLUES			
WERE THERE ANY GAPS IN YOUR ASSIGNMENT - DESCRIBE			
HAZARD DESCRIPTIONS			
COMMUNICATION PROBLEMS			
SUGGESTIONS FOR FUTURE OPERATIONS			

ATTACHMENTS: ☐ 214   ☐ TRANSPARENCY FORM
              ☐ 204   ☐ MAP
              ☐ OTHER DOCUMENTS

REVIEW QUESTIONS

1. A General Briefing should include a summary of the incident's

   _____ , _____ and

   _____ .

2. An Operational Briefing gives instructions to _____ .

3. The Operational Briefing will usually be conducted by the _____ .

4. List the five parts of the Operational Briefing.
   _____   _____
   _____   _____
   _____

5. The ICS form # _____ is used for the Operational Briefing.

6. Debriefing of the Crew Leader will generally be the responsibility of the

   _____ .

7. The purpose of debriefing the Crew Leader is to?
   _____

8. Debriefing topics should include:
   _____   _____
   _____   _____
   _____   _____
   _____   _____
   _____

9. What four items should the Crew Leader bring to the debriefing?
   _____   _____
   _____   _____

NOTES:

NOTES:

Chapter 9 - Hazardous Terrain Skills

HAZARDOUS TERRAIN SKILLS

OBJECTIVES

A. The student shall explain the procedures for traversing hazardous terrain in order to complete a search mission.

B. The student shall demonstrate the use of webbing and rope to rig a single point anchor system.

C. The student shall explain the definition of belay and it's use in land based SAR.

D. The student shall demonstrate tying a Prusik sling and it's use as a safety device.

E. The student shall demonstrate the tying and use of a Munter hitch.

F. The student shall combine the above skills, performing an evolution to demonstrate the use of these skills to allow a crew to safely traverse hazardous terrain.

G. The student shall demonstrate the construction of an improvised litter. This litter shall be suitable for the emergency transport of a victim. The litter shall be improvised using supplied equipment normally contained in a SAR Crew's (4 person) 24-hour packs. This litter is intended only for the emergency transport of a victim who is not seriously injured with no suspected spinal injury. (Local protocols should always be followed.)

TRAVERSING HAZARDOUS TERRAIN

Search crews face many challenges while completing a search mission assignment. The terrain within their search area can impose some degree of danger to the searchers. When faced with hazardous terrain the SAR TECH™ I/Crewleader III must have some technical rope skills to assure the safety of his/her search crew. Hazardous terrain can be described as a road embankment, a mountain side, an icy trail or simply low and steep angle terrain. High angle terrain requires advanced training and equipment and is not included in the SAR TECH™ I standard. It is important that some method of safety be used while ascending, descending or traversing hazardous terrain. Compared with the SAR TECH™ II pack, The SAR TECH™ I pack is a 24 hour ready pack with additional rope and rope hardware that will be useful for hazardous terrain. The additional equipment includes:

- 75 feet of static kernmantle rope, NFPA 1 person lifeline

- Two lengths of accessory or Prusik cord to be used as Prusik loops

- Two locking gate carabiners

- One section of 1" tubular webbing 20 feet in length

ROPE

The SAR TECH™ I, "24 hour" pack must contain 75 feet of one person lifeline rope. The National Fire Protection Association defines a one person lifeline as a rope that has a safe working load of not less than 300 pounds and shall be constructed of virgin fiber. The safe working load of a rope is calculated by dividing the minimum breaking strength of a rope by 15 which is commonly expressed as a 15 to 1 safety factor [15:1]. 7/16" static kernmantle rope is currently the most widely used rope for a one person lifeline. Static rope has a very low amount of stretch and works very well for low load ascending and descending when the fall factor is less than one. Accessory or so called 'Prusik cord' used to create Prusik loops, and even though it is smaller in diameter than the rope to which it is attached, it must be strong enough to support the intended load. Most Prusik loops are constructed from 6 mm to 8 mm kernmantle accessory or Prusik cord.

CARABINERS

Locking gate carabiners are preferred for search & rescue situations. Carabiners are constructed from aluminum alloy or steel. The steel design is much stronger but it is also heavier than aluminum. Rescue teams prefer the use of steel verses aluminum because of the additional strength and the resultant safety factor. The locking gate is important to ensure the gate of the carabiner does not open while loaded. Carabiners are used to connect the components of a rope system. They can also be used as friction devices.

WEBBING

Webbing is made of nylon or polyester and is either of tubular or flat construction. Tubular, spiral weave webbing is more commonly used for high angle operations. Webbing widths vary from 1/2 inch up to 2 inches with 1 inch width most commonly used by search and rescue crews. Two inch width webbing is now commonly used for constructing anchor slings and is more comfortable when used to tie an improvised harness.

SAFETY

A search mission in hazardous terrain requires the crewleader to be aware of hazardous areas. The crewleader may instruct crew members to don an improvised harness during the mission so that hazardous areas can be transversed safely. The safe use of any rope system requires knowledge of the systems weakest element so that an unsafe load is not placed upon it. The "safe working load" or safety capacity of a rope belay system can be calculated by dividing the minimum breaking strength of each in-

Chapter 9 - Hazardous Terrain Skills

dividual part in the system by fifteen. This is the 15:1 ratio described earlier. A rope that has a 4,500 pound minimum breaking strength has a safe working load of 300 pounds. [4500/15=300] The element of the system with the least safe working load represents the capacity of the entire system and is the amount of weight the entire system will safely hold. When you purchase rope, webbing, or other high angle hardware, find out from the manufacturer the minimum breaking strength of each item. Be aware that sharp bends and turns in rope or webbing decrease its minimum breaking strength. Sharp edges that might contact the rope or webbing must be padded to prevent sudden and accidental failure. Carabiners must be used to connect the components of a rope system so that heat; can be controlled to prevent failure that would be caused by excessive friction and stress when the system is loaded. Always tie a Figure 8 Knot or "Stopper Knot" **(See Figure 9.1)** in the standing, or bitter end, of the rope if the rope is either going to be used as a safety descent line or the rope is being fed through a braking device. This will assure that the person on the rope does not slip off the bitter end of the rope and will prevent the rope from being feed all the way through the braking device.

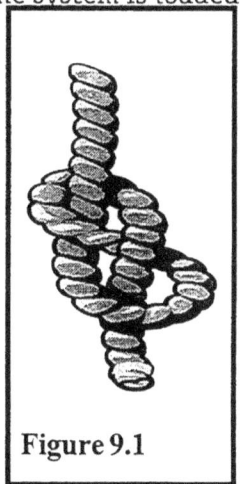

Figure 9.1

KNOTS AND HITCHES

The rope knots used in the SAR TECH™ I standard are also common to the SAR TECH™ II standard. However the SAR TECH™ I also has the "grapevine" (or "double fisherman's bend") and a two wrap (or four coil) "Prusik knot". The two hitches used in the SAR TECH™ 1 standard are the "tensionless anchor hitch" **(See Figure 9.2)** and the "Munter hitch". All of the knots and hitches used are demonstrated in the "Search and Rescue Fundamentals" text used in the NASAR *Fundamentals of Search and Rescue* (FUNSAR) course as well as several other rope rescue classes.

ANCHOR SYSTEM

An anchor is the attachment point for rope or webbing when rigging a rope system. Anchors must be "bomb-proof". This means the object used such as a tree or large boulder must be able to easily support the force of the load placed on the rope system. Only natural anchors

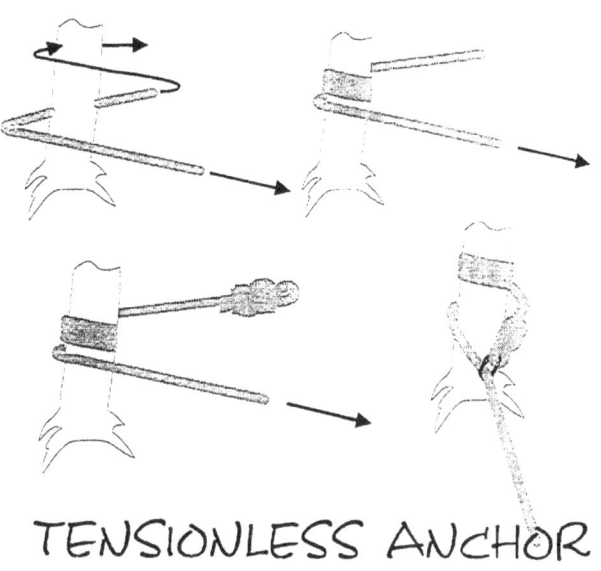

TENSIONLESS ANCHOR

Figure 9.2

will be covered in the SAR TECH™ I standard. A single point anchor can be established by tying a tensionless hitch.

A tensionless anchor hitch **(See Figure 9.2)** is tied by first tying a figure 8 on a bight knot in the running end of the rope. Make a minimum of three wraps or round turns around the object that has been chosen to be the anchor. For small diameter anchors use more wraps. Wrap from the bottom up if the anchor is above the load so that the wraps do not cross each other in the turns. Clip a locking gate carabiner into the figure 8 knot and connect it to the standing end (the end under tension) of the rope at the bottom of the spiral wraps or the standing end. Adjust the spiral wraps to decrease any slack in the wraps around the anchor object but leave enough slack at the running end to assure there is not a bend in the

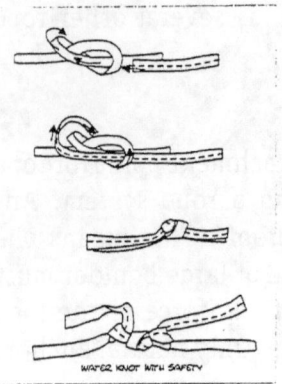

Figure 9.3

standing part of the rope where the carabiner connects. The wraps (also called 'round turns') around the anchor object must support the weight of the load. Another single point can be created by connecting the ends of a piece of webbing together with a water knot **(See Figure 9.3)** creating a sling.

The sling as shown in **(See Figure 9.4)** can then be wrapped or bighted around the anchor object and the ends connected together with a carabiner. A Figure 8 on a bight knot can be tied in the running end of a rope and clipped into the carabiner. In earlier times, rescue teams

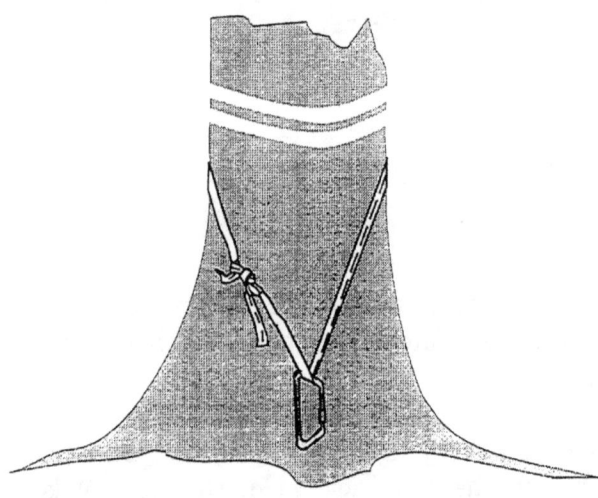

Figure 9.4

often used girth hitches when tying single point anchors. A girth hitch can create an excessive amount of friction causing the anchor sling to fail.

BELAY SYSTEM

For personal safety, a belay system must be used when a searcher is ascending, descending or traversing hazardous terrain. The belay system will usually consist of a rope attached to the searcher and then run through a braking device which is, in turn, attached to an anchor object. The braking device is controlled by another person known as the "belayer". The belayer has the responsibility to control the ascent or descent of the searcher and to prevent the searcher from falling. This is an important position and requires the belayer's constant attention. Searchers normally wear heavy packs which can easily over-balance them.

A searcher that is being belayed communicates to the belayer by using <u>standardized</u> verbal signals which every search leader needs to memorize. The searcher when ready to ascend or descend will say "on belay", which is the standard way of asking if the belayer is ready to catch the searcher if he/she were to fall. The belayer will respond with "belay on" meaning he/she is ready. The searcher then responds with "climbing" or "descending" to say he/she is beginning to go up or to go down. The belayer will acknowledge by saying "climb" or "descend". Once the searcher has finished the move and at a point of safety he/she says, "off belay" and the belayer will respond with, "belay off" meaning the searcher is no longer on belay and the belayer is no longer ready to catch the searcher.

A belay or friction device can be created using one of the carabiners carried in your pack. One technique is to tie a "Munter hitch". A secure anchor is tied by wrapping a piece of webbing one and one-half turns around the anchor object and connecting the ends with a water knot creating an anchor point. **(See Figure 9.4)** This also creates an internal loop that locks around the anchor object. Clip a large locking gate carabiner into the anchor sling. Adjust the water knot so the carabiner does not load on the knot when the webbing sling is loaded. The person being belayed dons an improvised harness, using his/her 20 foot section of 1 inch webbing. Tie a figure 8 on a bight in the end of the 75 foot section of rope and connect the loop with a carabiner to the improvised harness. Make sure the gate of the carabiner is locked.

The Munter hitch is tied by a two step method as shown in **(Figure 9.5)**. A small loop is made in the 75 foot section of rope. The section of the rope that is connected to the person

Chapter 9 - Hazardous Terrain Skills

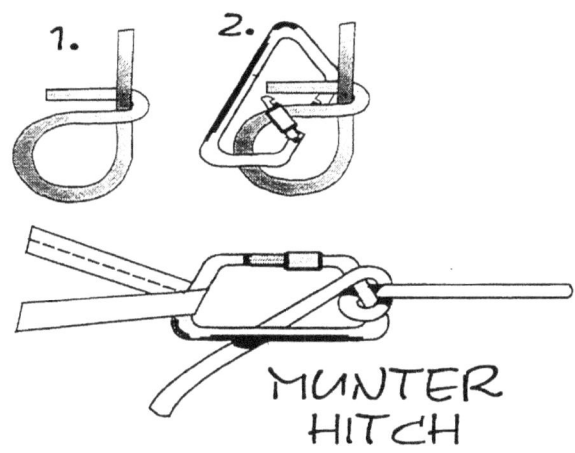

Figure 9.5

on belay is bighted around the other part of the rope that forms the loop.

Holding the loop you created in one hand, clip the carabiner into the loop and the section of the rope that is attached to the person on belay. Lock the gate of the carabiner. When loaded the rope will bight on itself around the carabiner creating friction or drag which allows the belay person to control the speed of the rope. A Munter hitch can be tied at any point in the rope and will provide friction when pulled in either direction. The belay person must always wear leather-palmed gloves because of possible rope burns if the rope is jerked through his/her hands.

It is important that any belay system be practiced on level ground to allow the belay person to become familiar with how the system operates. The belay person must face the anchor with the standing part of the rope in his/her strongest hand. This strong hand is the *braking hand*. The other hand is the *guide hand* and is placed on the running end of the rope and is the part that is connected to the person on belay. The belay person must not remove either hand from the rope while the searcher is being belayed. As the line is fed out the guide hand pulls out on the rope from the carabiner and the brake hand will approach the carabiner. When the brake hand gets within one foot of the carabiner, both sections of the rope are grasped by the guide hand and the brake hand slides backward on the standing part of the rope.

This can be done in a continuous motion and without interrupting the person on belay. Never let your brake hand leave the rope. If the person on belay needs to reverse direction, the Munter hitch can be reversed by simply pulling the rope back with the brake hand through the carabiner and feeding the rope to the carabiner with the guide hand. You must allow the Munter hitch knot to change direction. As the guide hand nears the carabiner, grasp both sides of the rope with your guide hand and slide your brake hand up to the carabiner without leaving the rope. Holding the rope with your brake hand, slide your guide hand back and continue the sequence. With practice this can be done in a continuous motion without hesitation or stopping.

Another method that is used is technically not a belay but is a safety that is controlled by the person on the rope and can be constructed by tying a Prusik around the rope. The Prusik loop is constructed by joining the two ends of an accessory cord together using a double fisherman's knot **(See Figure 9.6)** or a figure 8 bend. The double fisherman's knot is more commonly used but is the more difficult of the two to tie.

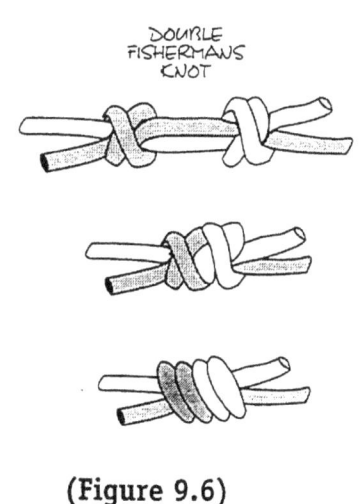

(Figure 9.6)

To tie the finished loop to the main rope **(See Figure 9.7)** place the Prusik loop between your two hands with the knot mid ways on one side. Pass the end of the loop under the belay rope and bring the end of the loop up vertically above the rope.

Take the opposite loop and pass it over the belay rope and through the vertical loop, passing it down and around the belay rope pulling the Prusik loop connecting knot through the vertical loop. Repeat this step one more time.

When completed, work the coils of the Prusik so the long loop end comes out the center of the coils. The Prusik loop is clipped in to the improvised harness with a carabiner. As the searcher ascends or descends along the belay or safety rope the Prusik is held in the searcher's hand and slid along the rope. In the event of a fall the Prusik is released from your hand. It should load and lock on the safety rope arresting the searcher's fall.

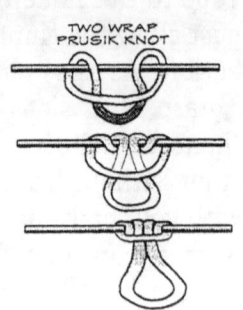

(Figure 9.7)

SUMMARY

The safety of the search crew must be constantly on the mind of the crewleader. Never attempt anything that you are not trained or equipped for. It is important to take the time to be assured the terrain can be traversed safely. Inspect all rope and hardware for damage before and after use.

PATIENT TRANSPORT

Searching and locating the lost subject does not always mean that the mission has been completed. If the subject has been injured, the SAR TECH™ I is now faced with the problem of getting the lost subject out of the area. Sometimes the subject will be able to walk out but often he/she will need some type of transportation. Before being moved the subject must be examined for injuries and other medical problems and appropriate actions must be taken to stabilize the problems that may be discovered. Life threatening injuries will require immediate medical attention. The results of your medical evaluation must be relayed to command as soon as possible. Some situations will require immediate transport. Most search crews will not have the medical equipment that is necessary to stabilize and properly package an injured subject for transport. **Local medical protocols must be adhered to in the field in extended transport situations.** A subject with suspected spinal injury must never be moved without proper equipment and training.

SAR TECH™ I PACK

The SAR TECH™ I pack contains items that can be used to improvise a stretcher for emergency transport.

- 75 ft. of one person lifeline rope
- 50 ft. of small diameter rope or cord
- 20 ft. of 1 inch tubular webbing
- 8 by 10 ft. shelter material

- 5 to 10 feet of duct tape
- Tracking stick

There may be other items carried in the 24 hour pack that may also be useful in stretcher construction. The usefulness of these items is only limited to the training you obtain in improvised stretcher construction and your imagination. The SAR TECH™ I should research and experiment with methods of improvised stretcher construction that are appropriate to the area terrain in which you usually search.

STRETCHER CONSTRUCTION

An improvised stretcher must provide safety, comfort, and security while the subject is being transported. Materials used in stretcher construction must be capable of supporting the weight of the subject you are transporting. A stretcher that requires constant stops to adjust its construction will only delay in the rapid transport of the subject.

Chapter 9 - Hazardous Terrain Skills

One method of stretcher construction is shown in **(Figure 9.9)**. It uses items contained in the 24 hour pack and 4 tracking sticks.

This stretcher is suitable for transporting someone who is fatigued or physically ill. It is not suitable for someone who is severally injured. You will need four tracking sticks that are capable of supporting the load, a sleeping bag and ground pad, 50 ft. of small diameter rope or cord and 20 ft. of 1 inch webbing. The tracking sticks must be placed on the ground parallel to each other 12 to 16 inches apart, depending on the size of the subject you will be transporting. Find the center of the 50 ft. section of cord and tie a clove hitch around one of the outside tracking sticks about 4 inches from

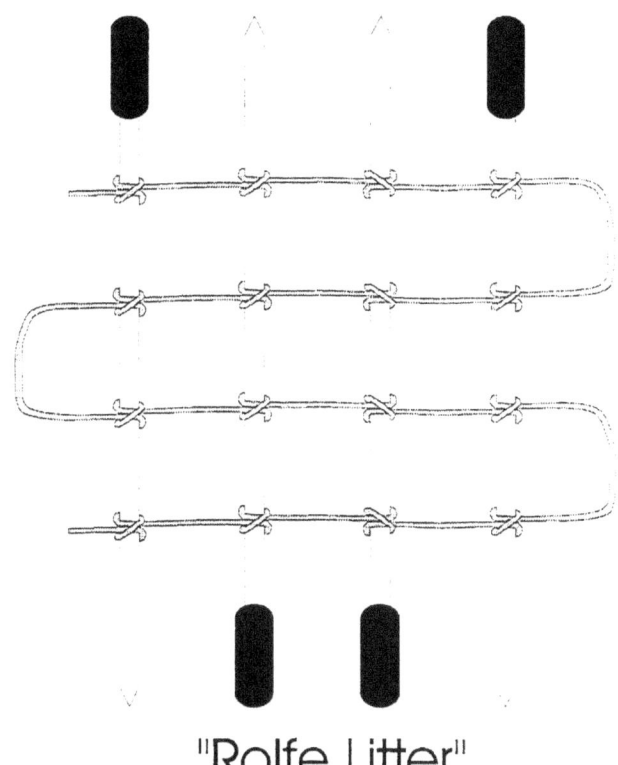

"Rolfe Litter"

Figure 9.9

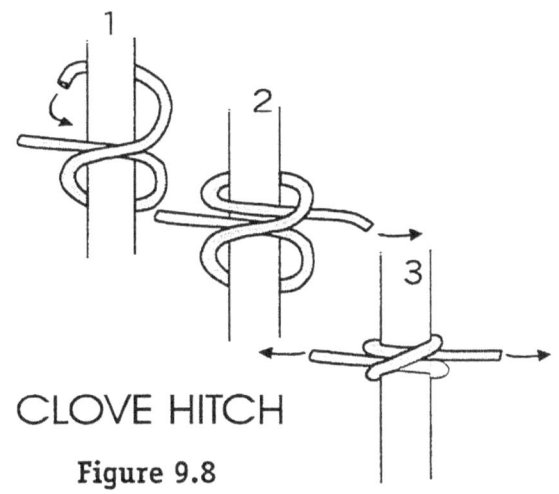

CLOVE HITCH

Figure 9.8

the center of the stick.

A clove hitch, as shown in figure 9-8, is tied by passing the running end of the cord over the pole and making one round turn. As the cord passes under the pole it should come under to your natural hand, either right or left. Pass the running end to the opposite side, over and under the pole again. As the running end of the cord comes under the pole for the second time, continue the turn passing under the cord where it crossed over the first round turn as you passed it to the opposite side.

Another method of tying a clove hitch is to form two counterclockwise loops, one in the right hand and one in the left hand. Now pass the right hand loop in front of the left hand loop, placing both loops together. Pass the two

loops over the tracking stick that you are using, adjust to the correct position and draw the knot tight.

Using the same tracking stick, tie another clove hitch with one half of the 50 ft. section of cord about 4 inches from the center of the stick on the opposite end. You should now have one tracking stick with two clove hitches spaced about 8 inches apart. With the four tracking sticks spaced evenly apart, tie two clove hitches around the second tracking about 8 inches apart keeping the second stick 12 to 16 inches from the first tracking stick. Continue the same procedure for the third tracking stick and the fourth tracking stick which will be on the outside. When completed you should have four parallel tracking sticks spaced 12 to 16 inches apart with two rows of clove hitches spaced four inches to each side of the center of each tracking stick. The final line of clove hitches must be tied at least 6 inches from the end of the tracking sticks to assure the cord does not slip off the sticks. Using one half of the 50 ft. section of cord, tie a clove hitch towards the handle of the fourth tracking stick about 8 inches from the adjoining clove hitch. On the same tracking stick, the other half of the cord is used to tie a clove hitch towards the tip of the tracking stick about 8 inches from its adjoining clove hitch. Clove hitches are again tied on the three other tracking sticks. The last clove hitches tied to the outside tracking stick used at the beginning must be secured with an overhand safety knot. When the stretcher is completed it should resemble a ladder. You should have several feet of cord left over after tying the last two clove hitches, and that extra cord can be used to secure the subject to the stretcher. This extra cord can also be used to create a back rest.

Place the ground pad and sleeping bag in the center of the stretcher parallel with the tracking sticks. The subject can be transported in or outside the sleeping bag, depending on the outside temperature. Due to the stretcher's short length the subject must sit in a reclining position during transport. Two additional tracking sticks or objects can be lashed to the two center tracking sticks, extending the length of the stretcher.

But regardless of how the stretcher is constructed, it is important that the proper hand location be used when raising and transporting the subject. The strength of the stretcher is from the 4 sections of cord connecting the tracking sticks and not the tracking sticks themselves. With two search crew members on each side, grasp the outside tracking sticks at the point where the clove hitches are tied at each end. The hand locations may need to be adjusted to balance the stretcher. Always remember the hand position must be at the point the clove hitch is tied around the tracking stick. Picking up on the tracking sticks between the clove hitches may cause the sticks to break. Always test the strength of the stretcher with an object of equal or greater weight than the subject who is to be transported. Experiment by using one of your team members. Don't experiment with an injured victim.

During transport the subject can support him/herself by locking the two outer tracking sticks under his/her arms or by placing a secured pack on the stretcher to lean on. The wrap around effect of the stretcher when lifted helps provide a lashing effect so that the victim tends to be held in the stretcher. For additional security the victim can be lashed to the stretcher using the 20 ft. section of 1 inch webbing. Proper lift procedures and vocal commands must be used to prevent injury to the searchers and subject during transport. Practice in constructing an improvised stretcher will allow you to learn methods of modifying the stretcher for varying needs of the subject.

SUMMARY

There are numerous methods that can be used to improvise a stretcher. The use of each method will depend on what is available to you when constructing the stretcher.

Of course rather than to build a stretcher in the field it is always better to use a device that is specifically designed for patient transport. But whether using a commercial stretcher or an improvised stretcher, never exceed your level of training. Improper techniques used during subject transport can be detrimental to both the subject and searchers.

A patient who needs and is medically able to endure rapid transport should be transported to the best of your ability. It is unfortunate that in many situations patients have suffered needlessly because of long delays in transport while waiting on the "proper" transport device. Using creativity and sound judgment, the SAR TECH™ I can provide this transportation and follow the medical protocols that are in force in your area.

GLOSSARY

anchor - A secure object that a rope system is attached to.

anchor point - Usually a single secure connection at an anchor.

ascending - The process of moving upward or climbing.

belay - A method of protecting a person attached to a rope from falling.

"bombproof" - A description of an anchor that is secure and can withstand the load that will be placed upon it.

brake hand (or natural hand) - Your dominant hand that holds the rope feeding into a friction device. Normally your right hand if you are right handed or left hand if you are left handed.

braking device (or descender) - A device that creates friction when attached to a rope.

clove hitch: two half hitches tied in the same direction that creates a securing hitch.

descending - The act of going in a downward motion such as walking down a hill.

guide hand - Non-dominant hand that is used to feed rope to or away from a break device.

lifeline - A rope that is designed to support a rated amount of weight to assure the safety of the individual attached to it.

Munter hitch - A sliding hitch that slips around a carabiner creating friction against itself.

Prusik knot - A friction knot when tied around a fixed rope that can be used as a safety aid when ascending.

Prusik loop - A section of rope tied together at its ends creating a loop for tying a prusik knot.

running end - The end of a rope that is used to tie a knot and is normally held in your natural hand.

safe working load - The load capacity of rope or rope hardware after the calculation of a safety factor. In rope, the minimum rated breaking strength is divided by fifteen for a safety factor of 15:1.

standing part of a rope - The part of a rope used to take the load.

standing end (or bitter end) - The opposite end of the running end.

stopper knot - A figure 8 knot that is tied a least one foot from the bitter end of a rope to prevent a person from accidentally sliding off the end of a rope.

REFERENCES

<u>High Angle Rescue Techniques</u>, by Tom Vines and Steve Hudson, Revised Edition, 1992.

<u>Search and Rescue Fundamentals</u>, by Cooper, Lavalla, and Stoffel, Third Edition, 1990.

<u>On Rope</u>, by Allen Padgett and Bruce Smith, First Edition, 1987.

REVIEW QUESTIONS

1. List the four items in the SAR TECH™ I ready pack that will be used for traversing hazardous terrain.

   _____   _____

   _____   _____

2. The one person life line carried in the SAR TECH™ I ready pack must have a safe working load of?

   _____

3. The safety ratio for the rope used in the hazardeous terrain station is _____ .

4. The new knots and/or hitches required for the SAR TECH™ I Evaluation are:

   _____   _____

   _____   _____

   _____

5. When ever using a rope as a life line, a Figure Eight _____ knot should always be tied in the "bitter end" of the rope.

6. Describe the wrapping of a Tensionless Hitch around an anchor when the load will be below the anchor point.

   _____

   _____

7. Describe a method for securing the rope to an anchor using the tubular webbing.

   _____

8. List two knots that can be used to join the ends of the accessory cord when forming a Prusik sling.

   _____   _____

9. Carabiners that are used in rescue applications should have a _____ as a safety feature.

10. The action of protecting individuals from a fall while they are on the rope is referred to as providing a:

    _____

11. List the two knots, hitches or wraps that are used by the SAR TECH™ I to accomplish the action described in Question 10.

    _____   _____

NOTES:

NOTES:

Chapter 10 - Stress Management ■ 139

STRESS MANAGEMENT

OBJECTIVES

A. The student shall explain the four (4) categories of symptoms relating to adverse stress reactions.

B. The student shall explain the four (4) ways to help prevent adverse stress reactions.

STRESS MANAGEMENT

Stress is a part of life. A moderate amount of stress is essential if an optimal level of alertness and performance are going to be maintained. Too little or too much stress generally has a negative impact on one's alertness and productivity. Every person involved in a search and rescue incident will experience stress. Stress is not something to be avoided. It is something to be managed. But, it must be managed properly in order to be dealt with effectively. If it is ignored or emotionally denied it may lead to an adverse stress reaction, diminished effectiveness during an operation and, possibly, "burn-out."

The stress experienced during a search and rescue incident is not the only stress experienced by the SAR personnel. The stress experienced during an incident is in addition to the stress brought to the SAR operation. Difficulties in interpersonal relationships, vocational tensions, environmental factors, fatigue, etc. all contribute to one's stress level. The amount of stress one experiences can heighten or hinder performance. The effects of stress on one's performance is unique to each individual.

This chapter's intention is to assist the SAR Tech I/Crewleader III in understanding the nature of stress and its impact on the individual. The SAR Tech I/Crewleader III must be able to appropriately manage stress and help others in their management of stress in order to ensure and maintain safety standards and optimal performance during an operation. Topics covered in this chapter are:

- to define the term "stress."
- to define and explain the role of "stressors."
- to identify three types of stressors.
- to identify and describe the four categories of symptoms relating to adverse stress reactions.
- to explain the four ways adverse stress reactions can be prevented.
- to describe when Critical Incident Stress Debriefing (CISD) may be necessary.

TOWARD AN UNDERSTANDING OF STRESS

Stress-free living is an impossibility. Stress, in moderate levels, can enhance one's life and performance. The term stress is defined by the Federal Emergency Management Agency (FEMA) as "a physical response of the body that occurs whenever we must adapt to changing conditions." (<u>Stress Management: Model Program for Maintaining Firefighter Well Being</u>. FEMA/USFA, Feb. 1991, p. 19)

Those things which effect an individual are known as stressors. There are three types of stressors.

(1) **Environmental Stressors** are those created by the incident context, i.e., terrain, weather, ICS (incident command system) issues and problems, decision making, etc.

(2) **Psychosocial Stressors** are those which come through interaction with others - communication problems, crew conflicts, interpersonal problems, etc.

(3) **Personality Stressors** are those which one creates for him/herself - reaction to criticism, inability to say no; inability to set personal limits, self-imposed guilt for not handling a situation beyond one's control, etc.[1]

Stress is a part of the search and rescue operation. Stress impacts one's performance during an operation. It is important that the SAR Tech I/Crewleader III be acutely aware of his personnel and the types of stress brought to, and being experienced during, an operation.

SYMPTOMS OF ADVERSE STRESS REACTIONS

The SAR Tech I/Crewleader III must be aware of the symptoms produced by an adverse stress reaction. It should be noted that "Emergency responders [tend to] suppress their fear, ignore clues of danger and press on with a belief they cannot be harmed."[2] This ability, which can be a major asset during a critical operation, is also the emergency personnel's greatest liability. The health and safety of operational personnel is of the highest priority. Therefore, it is essential that the four categories of adverse symptoms of stress be known, recognized, and addressed with utmost urgency before, during and after an operation.

Category I: Cognitive Symptoms are a person's ability to think clearly. This may be evidenced by an inability to make judgments and decisions, lack of ability to conceptualize alternatives or prioritize tasks, confusion, inability to evaluate one's own functioning, etc.

Category II: Psychological Symptoms are a person's psychological demeanor. This may be evidenced by emotional mood swings, irritability, depression, apathy, anger, hyper-excitability, lack of patience, etc.

Category III: Physical Symptoms or physical characteristics. This may be evidenced by hypochondria, loss of energy, loss of sleep, appetite irregularities, gastrointestinal distress, chills, sweats, etc.

Category IV: Behavioral Symptoms: This may be evidenced by excessive fatigue, hyperactivity, inability to express one's self verbally or in writing, etc.[3]

It is essential that the SAR Tech I/Crewleader III be able to identify and assess the stress level of crew members in order to ensure their health and safety. Remember that each crew member is already experiencing stress prior to the incident and that this stress is compounded by the incident. This is especially true when it is an extended operation, involves children, taking place in adverse weather and terrain, when foul play is suspected or involved, etc. The key to preventing an adverse stress reaction is to *proactively* manage stress during the operation.

MANAGING STRESS DURING AN OPERATION

Stress management must be taken seriously during an operation. The SAR Tech I/Crewleader III must be able to identify symptoms of stress in one's self and others. There are four ways that one can assist in preventing an adverse stress reaction.

1. Establish appropriate ground rules for personnel during the search. Make sure each members' level of training and skill are ascertained and appropriate responsibilities assigned. Inexperienced SAR personnel can receive valuable "on the job training," but be sure that they are being properly supervised.
2. Recognize that all people have limits. These limits must be acknowledged and respected. Be alert to mental, emotional and physical fatigue. Make sure that appropriate rest is provided and that each member's intake of calories and liquids is adequate. If you are working with volunteers remember that they may have to work their regular job the next day.
3. Maintain realistic expectations. SAR personnel are human. One cannot expect himself or others to act in superhuman ways.
4. Recognize stress, allow individuals to discuss frustrations, express limitations and respond in an affirming and encouraging manner.

Preventing problems in the field requires that the Crewleader be an astute observer of the crew members. Take breaks, discuss matters other than the operation, make sure assignments are appropriate to a person's technical skill and training, provide oversight, teach and instruct rather than criticize and reprimand, ensure that each member takes time off from the operation, and be willing to remove SAR personnel from the operation rather than compromise the health and safety of the individual and crew.

Search operations involve stress. The amount of stress can be managed effectively by the SAR Tech I/Crewleader III.

Should I Contact CISD

Critical Incident Stress Debriefing is a valuable resource and is appropriate when an acute or unusual emotional reaction to stress is experienced which interferes with one's ability to function at the scene or later; according to Jeffrey Mitchell.[4] CISD may be appropriate when a disaster is involved, a young child is involved or other extreme situations. CISD is a tool which aids the SAR personnel in dealing with the emotional stresses resulting from an incident. It encourages personnel to:

(1) Share their feelings about an incident and allow a facilitator to assess them.
(2) Discuss the signs and symptoms of stress with a trained facilitator.
(3) Develop a plan of action with a facilitator, including the need for further debriefing or counseling if appropriate.[5]

Conclusion

SAR personnel must fulfill a multiplicity of roles and responsibilities as well as the stress brought to the incident which sometimes overloads one's capability to cope. The SAR Tech I/Crewleader III must be able to effectively identify symptoms of stress and take appropriate action to relieve stress in order to ensure the health and safety of each crew member. The SAR Tech I/Crewleader III who *proactively* manages stress will be able to perform optimally during an operation and make a significant contribution to its overall effectiveness.

1 Adapted from Jeffrey T. Mitchell and Grady Brady. Emergency Services Stress:
   Guidelines for Preserving the Health and Careers of Emergency Services Personnel (Englewood Cliffs: Brady, 1990)

2 David Freeman, Maintaining Our Resources. (n.p. Critical Incident Stress Debriefers of Florida, n.d.)

3 Adapted from SAR Fundamentals, Pg. 202

4 SAR Fundamentals, Pg. 204

5 Ibid, Pg 204

Chapter 10 - Stress Management

REVIEW QUESTIONS

1. List the four categories of adverse symptoms of stress.

   _____   _____

   _____   _____

2. List the four steps that should be taken to manage stress.

   _____   _____

   _____   _____

3. _____ is a program which has been developed to help individuals cope with emotional stress that may result from a search mission.

NOTES:

SUMMARY

Introduction to Search and Rescue (ISAR) course was designed as the basic course for all SAR personnel. It provides the basic SAR concepts and procedures for all sections of the Incident Command System during a search mission. *Fundamentals of Search and Rescue* (FUNSAR course was intended to train the individual as a member of a SAR crew within the operations section. ISAR, followed by certification as SAR TECH™ III and FUNSAR, followed by certification as SAR TECH™ II helps to insure that qualified SAR personnel are available for search operations.

Employing the "weak link" theory, the knowledge and abilities of each individual can have an effect on each phase of the search mission. The Incident Commander will write the Incident Objectives, the Planning Section Chief will develop a plan, the Operations Chief will devise the tactics, and the Logistics Section Chief will assure all resources are provided. The success of the search effort rests on each individual, in each position knowing their job, and performing it to the best of their ability. The best of Incident Objectives and Incident Action Plans will have little success, if the individual responders are not able to accomplish the tasks!

Advanced Search and Rescue (ADSAR), followed by certification as SAR TECH™ I/Crewleader III represents the next step in ensuring the success of the search operation. Assuming that we have capable individuals and resources, they will need an equally capable leader to accomplish their assignments. There are no "born leaders"! Each of us is capable of becoming a leader. When given the knowledge and tools of the job, and the self-confidence to apply them, each of us is capable of realizing the potential within.

As you review the ADSAR Course, recall your experiences. With whom have you worked in the past? How did this individual affect you? If the effect was positive, why was it so? If the effect was negative, why was that so? How will you deal with others, some of whom you may never have met prior to the mission, when faced with the challenges of the mission. Will you inspire others? Will your crew have confidence in you as the Crewleader? Your success, will be their success. Your failure, will be their failure. You will be responsible. ADSAR and the SAR TECH™ I/Crewleader III Evaluation are intended to give you the knowledge and self-confidence to lead others.

Once you have completed the ADSAR Course and the SAR TECH™ I/Crewleader III Evaluation, take note of the list of referenced texts in the SAR TECH™ I/Crewleader III Standards. The authors that contributed to this text, felt that the reference material was essential to their understanding of the topics each would be contributing. Much of the information contained in this text, was gleaned from these references. Each contributor was chosen because each is a successful Crewleader in their own right. Follow their lead, and review the references. The more knowledge you have and the more skills you can employ, the higher your level of confidence in yourself.

INCIDENT COMMAND

The first step in the success of the search operation is for each person in each position to accomplish their assignment. Expectations are placed on individuals and it is important that everyone know what is expected of them. Individuals perform better when they know where and how they "fit into" the overall picture. As the Crewleader, you will be looked upon by your crew to have the answer for the question "where do I fit in?". Understanding the "big picture" will give you the confidence to answer the question.

Simply put, ICS organizes all of the personnel into a singular effort to resolve the incident. This organizational system identifies functions that will resolve the incident and assigns tasks to be done to accomplish the functions. ICS expands and contracts in a modular fashion.

When a function is deemed essential to resolving the incident, a functional "module" is established. When that function is no longer essential, then the module is demobilized. A 5:1 manageable span-of-control governs ICS with additional modules of the system activated when necessitated by the increasing work load as the response to the incident grows. The organizational functions are broad in scope:

- Establishing the goals (objectives) for resolving the incident is the function of the Command Section.

- Determining the tactics that will be employed and identifying the tasks to achieve the goals is the function of the Operations Section.

- Recommending strategies and iidentifying the resources that can accomplish the tasks is the function of the Plans Section.

- Providing support for the resources is the function of the Logistics Section.

- Determining who will pay for resolving the incident is the function of the Finance Section.

Each of these Sections is supervised by a Section Chief who is ultimately responsible for the function they have been assigned. When the work load becomes more than the Section Chief can efficiently handle, a subordinate is identified that will handle tasks within that particular function. When the chain-of-command has been established, task assignments generally move down the chain and reports move up the chain. Using the chain-of-command, ICS tracks the progress in resolving the incident.

Here is how the system works:

The initial Incident Commander will determine what should be done initially to resolve the incident. The initial IC will determine the tactics and strategies and assign resources in order to accomplish this initial response. Should the initial response not resolve the incident, the initial IC will determine what additional resources are necessary to resolve the incident. This information is documented on ICS Form #201.

When it becomes apparent that the incident will require more resources than that of the initial response, an Incident Action Plan will be developed to employ the additional resources effectively. The Incident Action Plan will be documented on a set of five forms, ICS Forms #202, #203, #204(s), #205, and #206. In addition to general information (i.e.: the name of the incident, date, operations period, etc.) each form documents specific information.

Form #202: Contains the objectives that should be accomplished in order to resolve the incident. These objectives should be attainable so that tactics can be utilized, and measurable so that progress in resolving the incident can be known. This form is completed by the Incident Commander.

Form #203: Contains the position assignments of the various personnel that will be responsible for the functions that have been deemed essential for resolving the incident. This form is completed by the Planning Section Chief.

Form #204(s): Contain the task assignments that will move down the chain-of-command. This form will be used to document all tasks for all positions in the ICS. These forms are completed by the Planning Section Chief (or designee) based on the Work sheet (ICS Form #215) which is completed by the Operations Section Chief.

Form #205: Contains the radio frequencies that will be utilized, and who will be authorized to communicate on each of the frequencies. This form is completed by the Logistics Section Chief.

Form #206: Contains directions for handling medical emergencies involving personnel who are working to resolve the incident. This form is completed by the Logistics Section Chief.

This systematic method of planning and organization assures the search is conducted in an efficient and effective manner with the focus of finding the lost subject being the primary goal.

SMALL UNIT LEADERSHIP

There are no "born leaders" but each of us is capable of becoming a leader. Acquiring and practicing the skills of being a Crewleader will give you the confidence in yourself to inspire and motivate your Crew.

Make an honest appraisal of yourself as a leader, and determine which of the following leadership traits you currently possess, and which traits you need to "work on". You may want to ask others for feedback.

- Courage
- Bearing
- Decisiveness
- Dependability
- Endurance
- Enthusiasm
- Humility
- Humor
- Initiative
- Integrity
- Judgment
- Justice
- Knowledge
- Tact
- Loyalty
- Selflessness

We all have some of the leadership traits, but few of us will have all. We all have a tendency to practice things we feel we are good at doing, few of us are willing to practice (and try to improve) those things we feel are lacking.

Which of the following leadership principles do you currently employ, and which do you need to "work on"? Again, ask others for feedback.

- Self-improvement, self-realization
- Knowledgeable and tactically efficient
- Seek responsibility, take responsibility
- Making sound and timely decisions
- Setting examples
- Care about the people you lead
- Sharing information
- Creating responsibility in others
- Instructing, supervising and supporting
- Creating a team
- Matching the Crew to the assignment

Which management theory do you feel the most comfortable employing? Are you rigid in your approach, directing those around you in tasks and expecting them to perform with little input from you? Or, are you flexible in your approach, motivating those around you, and inspiring them to perform? Conflict Management is effective, and has been employed successfully for years. Situational Management has more risks and is sometimes more successful. At times a situational manager must create a little conflict to get the job done!

Which supervisory technique will you employ in order for your Crew to accomplish the mission? Both types of Managers, Conflict and Situational, will have to supervise the work of their Crew in order to assure the job gets done. Successful supervision is accomplishing a task through the efforts of others. Which of the following elements of supervision do you need to improve in yourself to assure that you and your Crew are successful?

- Communication
- Teamwork
- Involvement
- Initiative
- Positive Supervision
- Set Standards
- Control Measures
- Performance Feedback

FITNESS FOR THE CREWLEADER

Not only will your Crew judge you by your ability to manage the Crew's efforts on the mission, you will also be judged by your ability to perform in the field. In some cases, the Crewleader may be called upon to prepare the Crew for response into the field. If the Crew's success is measured by the "weak link theory", the Crew's success should not be hampered by an weak and out-of-shape Crewleader!

CREW SAFETY

It will be the Crewleader's responsibility to assure that their Crew operates safely and efficiently while in the field. Each Crewleader should operate with the attitude that the mission is a "round trip ticket" - everyone that responds with the Crew will return from the field.

Review the influences that are likely to affect the Crew's safety while in the field. Some safety issues will be area-specific, others are generalized concerns.

READY PACK

Additional equipment and supplies are included in the SAR TECH™ I/Crewleader III Ready Pack enable to the Crewleader to better support the Crew. Some equipment will be specific to skills taught in the ADSAR Course and evaluated during the SAR TECH™ I/Crewleader III Certification Evaluation, other equipment and supplies were added to support the Crew. The SAR TECH™ I/Crewleader III Ready Pack is recommended as a minimum requirement for Crewleaders, you may want to add additional equipment and supplies that are specific for the area(s) in which you will be operating.

MAPS, SYMBOLOGY, AND NAVIGATION

The success of the search effort will depend on getting crews to the areas that need to be searched, having them accomplish the tasks they have been assigned, then having them return to base camp for debriefing. The Crewleader will be responsible for knowing where the Crew is located, getting the Crew to the area of operations, then getting the Crew to the pick up location. Many electronic location and navigation (GPS) devices are available on the market. Some of these have become more affordable and user friendly in the past few years. All GPS units have the draw back of operating on batteries, (which can go dead) and of "listening" to satellites (which can be blocked by vegetation and terrain) in order to work. The Crewleader will always need to be able to fix the Crew's location without the relying on the use of a GPS unit.

Successful orienteering and navigation in a variety of terrain, containing a variety of vegetation, during any weather, and, at any time of day or night will require the Crewleader to possess and apply skills in many different situations. Many SAR Units not only operate in their own familiar areas, but travel to other areas where they are less familiar. Orienteering and navigation skills require practice in order to be mastered.

Many people use orienteering compasses that can be adjusted for magnetic declination. Are you prepared in the event that your compass is lost, or for some reason becomes inoperable? Do you have a backup compass? Is it also adjustable? Prepare your map with the grid lines (which you will need for orienting yourself) and then draw in the magnetic north lines. You can still use the orienteering compass adjusted for magnetic declination, and you have the option of using the prepared map should your primary compass fail. It is much easier to prepare the map at base camp, than to try and prepare it in the field.

Prior to going into the field during training exercises, practice reading the contour lines on the topographic map and formulate a mental "picture" of how the terrain will appear (and change) as you travel. Also note what features may appear on the terrain (buildings, bridges, roads, etc.) and how they are indicated (symbols) on the map. Your path may begin at a trail head on a road, proceed along a ridge line and through a saddle, then go down a draw to the creek. Once you have the mental picture, travel by terrain association, comparing what you actually see to the mental picture you formulated, and check it with the map. Most all topographic maps have contour lines! The contour intervals may be different, but they will appear similarly on the map. Terrain association is a skill that can be learned and practiced anywhere and then applied anywhere! Personnel from the "low lands" navigate very well in the mountains. Be aware of how you arrived in the area. What roads did you take to get where you started from? Where was the sun, or moon? From which direction was the wind blowing, or from where were the clouds moving. This information may become useful when you later have to fix your location.

SEARCH TECHNIQUES AND TACTICS

Your ultimate role as a Crewleader will be to conduct a search of an area. You will be asked to provide as high a POD as possible for your assigned area. When you return from your mission, you will be asked how successfully you accomplished your mission so that plans may be made for the rest of the operation. You may be given a "target POD" for your Crew to accomplish. Once you are in the area, it will be up to you how you configure your Crew to accomplish the task. How will you make the maximum use of the resource you have been entrusted to lead? What techniques will you employ to cover the area within the time frame you have been given? You will be expected to know where your Crew operated, how much area you and the Crew covered and how well the area was searched. The more accurate your debriefing, the better the plan for the next operational period.

You may have to instruct your Crew Members in scanning vs. observing an area. You will have to configure your Crew to sweep through the area, with the appropriate critical separation to achieve the "target POD". Should you find a clue in your assigned area, you may have to change your tactics from sign-cutting to a more thorough tactic to follow up on the clue. As the Crewleader you will be expected to select and employ the search techniques and tactics that best accomplish the task you have been assigned to accomplish. When you return to base and are debriefed, will you be able to justify the search techniques and tactics you employ?

BRIEFING AND DEBRIEFING

As we discussed in the Incident Command section, tasks and task assignments move down the Chain-of-Command and situation reports move up the Chain-of-Command. Briefing of personnel is used to assign tasks, and Debriefing of personnel is used for situation reports.

There are two types of Briefings:

General Briefing

The purpose of the General Briefing is to make everyone involved in the incident aware of general purpose information. The General Briefing will consist of a summary of the past situation (what has occurred thus far), present (what is currently being done to mitigate the incident) and future (what we anticipate will occur in the near and distant future). Information for the General Briefing comes from the Incident Action Plan (IAP) specifically ICS Forms #202 (Incident Objectives) and #203 (Organization Assignment List), and ICS Form #215 (Operations Work sheet).

Operational Briefing

The purpose of the Operational Briefing is to make the individual Crewleaders aware of what will be expected of their Crew, specifically. The information for the Operational Briefing is contained on the ICS Form(s) #204 and consists of 5 parts:

1. Situation - as it applies to the resource
2. Mission - what the crew is expected to accomplish
3. Execution - explicit instructions about where and how to search
4. Administration and Logistics - in support of the Crew to accomplish their assignment.
5. Communications and Command - what frequencies to be used, and who is responsible for what.

After the Crewleader has received the Crew's assignment, the Crewleader will meet with the Crew and review the assignment so that all individuals are aware of what will be expected of them for the Operations Period. After briefing their Crew, each Crewleader should "brief back" with the individual that briefed the Crewleader. This "brief back" assures that the Crewleader understands exactly what is expected of the Crew. Specific problems with the assignment may have been identified by the Crew and the "brief back" allows the Crewleader the opportunity to make the Operations Chief aware of potential problems before they occur.

Debriefing

The purpose of Debriefing is to make the Operations Section and the Planning Section aware of the situation. The information for the Crew's debriefing is contained in the ICS Form #214 (Unit Log). The information from the ICS Form #214 will be used for the IAP (Forms #202, #215, and #204's), which will be used to brief the Crews for the next Operational period. Accurate debriefing of the Crews will allow for accurate planning for the rest of the operation.

HAZARDOUS TERRAIN SKILLS

In depth instruction of technical rope techniques is beyond the scope of this class, and of the SAR TECH™ I/Crewleader III Evaluation. The intent of providing the ADSAR Student and SAR TECH™ I/Crewleader III Candidate with information concerning Hazardous Terrain Skills is to give the individual an easy-to-remember, and easy-to-execute traverse for crossing difficult areas as safely as possible.

There may well be several ways in which to configure a traverse utilizing the equipment contained in the SAR TECH™ I/Crewleader III Ready Pack. It should be noted that there is no singularly "correct" traverse for any situation. The traverse outlined in this text is identified as a measurable standard for the SAR TECH™ I/Crewleader III Certification Evaluation and will be evaluated during the SAR TECH™ I/Crewleader III Certification Evaluation.

Considerations for equipment and execution of the Hazardous Terrain evolution includ:

1. That only one person (the SAR TECH™ I/Crewleader III) is required to set up the traverse.
2. That the SAR TECH™ I/Crewleader III could easily instruct the Crew in how to use the traverse.
3. That the skills required for the Crew Members to use the traverse were skills including in SAR TECH™ II Certification.
4. The equipment requirements where easy to pack and light weight enough to be included in the SAR TECH™ I/Crewleader III Ready Pack.
5. The equipment met (or exceeded) the National Fire Protection Administration (NFPA) Guidelines for single-rescuer lifeline.

For those Students who are not familiar with technical rope techniques, the traverse taught in ADSAR will require periodic practice to execute the evolution in a variety of conditions. For those Students who are more familiar with technical rope techniques and equipment, your expertise and training should guide you in determining how you and your Crew will traverse a hazard.

STRESS IN SAR CREWS

Post Traumatic Stress is defined as stress caused by experiences outside the realm of normal human experience. Everyone should recognize that the average SAR mission is outside the realm of normal human experience! "Normal" people don't get out of bed, in the middle of the night, to go out a look for someone that they don't even know!! We may train for many hours, days and months for the mission and still not be truly prepared for everything that we will encounter.

It will be the responsibility of the SAR TECH™ I/Crewleader III to assure that the Crew accomplishes its mission. Everyone, including the Crewleader will be operating in a stressful environment. Everyone, including the Crewleader will experience a measure of Post Traumatic Stress, which will be "normal". How we deal with the stress will determine whether Post Traumatic Stress becomes a Post Traumatic Stress Disorder.

The effective Crewleader will make the effort to recognize stress in themselves and in their Crew Members, and then, take steps to mitigate that stress.

Course Summary

SITUATION

You have arrived at base camp to assist in the search for a lost person. When you signed in on the ICS Form #211, you indicated that you are a SAR TECH™ I/Crewleader III.

The Incident Commander has written the Incident Objectives for the operations period on the ICS Form #202.

The Operations Chief has written tasks to accomplish the Incident Objectives on the ICS Form #215. The Ops. Chief has also indicated what Type of Resource should be assigned to each task.

The Resource Unit Leader in the Planning Section has assigned you as a Crewleader of a three-person Type I Search Crew. The Planning Section Chief has supervised the preparation of the assignments on ICS Form #204(s).

The Logistics Section Chief has provided the information on radio frequencies to be used (ICS Form #205), medical procedures to be followed in the event one of your Crew is injured (ICS Form #206), transportation information, and other support information (ICS Form #203) for your use as a Crewleader.

The next General Briefing is scheduled for 1700 hrs.

At the General Briefing, the Planning Section Chief introduces the Incident Commander. The IC reviews the incident objectives and thanks you for your assistance in resolving this incident. The Planning Section Chief then reports the past situation, present situation and future predictions about the search. This information has been compiled by the Situation and Documentation Unit Leaders. The Operations Section Chief is introduced and gives you a report on what will be accomplished during this operational period. The weather forecast will be updated and any general safety information will be reviewed. Copies of the subject profile, track description and picture of the subject is distributed.

You will be introduced as a Crewleader and the members of your crew will be introduced.

Now begins your job as the Crewleader!

Instruct you Crew to prepare themselves and their equipment for deployment, and give them a time to assemble for a crew briefing.

You will receive an Operational Briefing from the Operations Section Chief (or designee, i.e.: a Division Supervisor in large incidents) and review the ICS Form #204 for your assignment. You may be given a map overlay of your assignment, an ICS Form #214 to document your crew's actions and will be told when and who will debrief you after finishing your assignment.

When your Crew has assembled, review your mission assignment, assign members individual responsibilities and make certain they understands what is expected of them. Assure that each member of the Crew has the equipment and supplies that will support them during the mission.

After briefing your Crew, you return to your supervisor who briefed you, and brief back the assignment. This assures you, the Crew and your supervisor the assignment is completely understood.

Load your Crew in the assigned vehicle(s) quickly and efficiently and travel to your assigned drop off point.

Be sure your Crew's activities are documented. Perhaps you will keep the ICS Form #214 and compete it as necessary, or you may have assign this task to a Crew Member. In either case, make certain that your Crew's activities are documented.

Once you are in the field, assure that you and your Crew are at the correct "drop off" point. If so, proceed to your assigned search segment. If not, still proceed to your assigned segment in the quickest manner possible. This may require you to map out a travel route in the field. How irritated will you be when you must correct this mistake? How will your Crew react, not only to the mistake, but to your reaction to the mistake. How will you deal with your stress, and the stress experienced by the Crew?

When you reach your assigned search segment, determine how best to accomplish the objectives outlined on the ICS Form #204. Configure your Crew so that you will attain the highest POD. Keep track of the area that your Crew searches, and determine the overall percentage of the assigned segment that you and your Crew have searched.

Keep track of where your Crew is located within your assigned search segment. What will you escape route be in the event you have to abandon your mission quickly? Report to the Command Post at the predetermined time intervals, so that Operations is aware of your progress as you search your segment.

When your assignment is completed, gather your Crew and proceed to your pickup point.

When you have returned to the Command Post, be ready to debrief. Thank your Crew Members for the job they have done and offer them the opportunity to participate in the debriefing. Relate what you and your Crew have accomplished, using the information on the ICS Form #214. This is your opportunity to offer suggestions and recommendations as to what you think should be done during future operations periods.

Now that you are "out-of-service", take some time to reflect on your mission and for self critique. What did you do well, and, what could you have done better? Talk with some of the other Crewleaders, and personnel from other Crews. Relating your experiences, and hearing the experiences of others helps in the learning process, and, helps mitigate your own stress. Give yourself time to "get away" from the operation, so that you can return physically and *mentally* refreshed.

**We hope this text and the
ADSAR course has increased
your effectiveness as a
member of a SAR Crew
and a SAR Crewleader.**

"That Others May Live"

www.ingramcontent.com/pod-product-compliance
Lightning Source LLC
Chambersburg PA
CBHW081354230426
43667CB00017B/2831